how about making
an auto-respon'
course - Ca

MW00415355

The Master Mind
Or
The Key To
Mental Power
Development & Efficiency
by Theron Q Dumont

Advanced Thought Publishing Co.

Chicago, ILL

Janice & Mel's
Life Transformation Publishing
2013

ISBN-13: 978-1490991436

ISBN-10: 1490991433

Janice & Mel's
Life Transformation Publishing
www.lifetransformationpublishing.com
2013

Specializing in Transforming Lives!

Check out our other titles at the end
of the book!

CONTENTS

The Master Mind

In this book there will be nothing said concerning metaphysical theories or philosophical hypotheses; instead, there will be a very strict adherence to the principles of psychology. There will be nothing said of "'spirit" or "soul"; but very much said of "mind." There will be no speculation concerning the question of "what is the soul," or concerning "what becomes of the soul after the death of the body." These subjects, while highly important and interesting, belong to a different class of investigation, and are outside of the limits of the present inquiry. We shall not even enter into a discussion of the subject of "what is the mind"; instead, we shall confine our thought to the subject of "how does the mind work."

For the purposes of the present consideration of the subject before us, we shall rest content with the fundamental postulate that "Every man or woman has a mind," and the corollary that when an intelligent man or woman speaks of "myself," he or she is conscious that his or her "mind" has a more intimate relation to that "self" than has his or her "body." The "'body" is usually recognized as "belonging to" the "self," while the "mind" is usually so closely identified with the "self" that it is difficult to

4

distinguish them in thought or expression.

Many philosophers and metaphysicians have sought to tell us "just what" the mind is; but they usually leave us as much in doubt as before the so-called explanation. As the old Persian poet has said, we usually "come out the door in which we went," in all such discussions and speculations concerning the nature of mind, or "just what mind really is." We can, and do, know much about how the mind works, but we know little or nothing about what the mind really is. But, for that matter, so far as practical purposes are concerned, it makes very little difference to us just what the mind is, providing we know just how it works, and how it may be controlled and managed.

What the Mind Is

A well-known psychologist has well said: "It used to be the fashion to begin psychologies with a discussion concerning the material or immaterial nature of the mind. It has been well said that psychology is no more bound to begin by telling what the mind is, than physics is obliged to start by settling the vexed question as to what matter is. Psychology studies the phenomena of mind, just as physics investigates those of matter.

Fortunately, phenomena do not change with our varying views as to what things really are. The phenomena of electricity remain the same whether we consider it a fluid, a repulsion of molecules, or vibrations of the ether. If a man hold the strange theory that electricity was a flock of invisible molecular goats that pranced along a wire with inconceivable rapidity, he would still have to insulate the wires in the same way, generate the current in the same way. A strong discharge would kill him as quickly as if he held a different theory. In short, his views of the ultimate substance of electricity would in nowise change its phenomena.

If any materialist should hold that the mind was nothing but the brain, and that the brain was a vast aggregation of molecular sheep herding together in various ways, his hypothesis would not change the fact that sensation must precede perception, memory, and thought; nor would the laws of association of ideas be changed, nor would the fact that interest and repetition aid memory cease to hold good. The man who thought his mind was a collection of little cells would dream, imagine, think, and will; so also would he who believed his mind to be immaterial. It is very fortunate that the same mental phenomena occur, no matter what theory is adopted. Those who like to study the puzzles as to what mind and matter really are, must go to metaphysics. Should we ever find that salt, arsenic, and many things else, are the same substances with a different molecular arrangement, we should still not use them interchangeably.

Another well-known psychologist, speaking upon the same subject, calls our attention to the custom of a celebrated teacher of psychology who usually began his first lecture by bidding his pupils to "think about something, your desk, for example"; he who would then add: "Now think of that which thinks about the desk"; and then, after a few moments concluding the remark with the statement: "This thing which thinks about the desk, and about which you are now thinking, is the subject matter of our study of psychology."

The psychologist above mentioned has said further on this subject: "The mind must either be that which thinks, feels, and wills, or it must be the thoughts, feelings, and acts of will of which we are conscious—mental facts, in one word. But what can we tell about that which thinks, feels, and wills, and what can we find out about it? Where is it? You will probably say, in the brain. But, if you are speaking literally, if you say that it is in the brain, as a pencil is in the pocket, then you must mean that it takes up room, that it occupies space, and that would make it very much like a material thing. In truth, the more carefully you consider it, the more plainly you will see what thinking men have known for a long time—that we do not know and cannot learn anything about the thing which thinks, and feels, and wills. It is beyond the range of human knowledge. The books which define psychology as the science of mind have not a word to say about that which thinks, and feels, and wills. They are entirely taken up with these thoughts and feelings and acts of the will—mental facts, in a word—trying to tell us what they are, and to arrange them in classes, and tell us the circumstances or conditions under which they exist. It seems to me that it would be better to define psychology as the science of the experience, phenomena, or facts of the mind, soul, or self—of mental facts, in a word."

And, so in this book, we shall not invade the field of metaphysics or the region of philosophy, with the endless discussions of "about it and about" concerning the "just what is" of the soul, self, or mind. Rather shall we dwell contentedly in the safer region of "mental facts," and speak only of the "just how to do things" with the mind, based upon the discovery of "just how the mind works" made by advanced psychology. This is the method of the Pragmatic Plan now so favored by modern thinkers—the plan which is concerned with the "how," rather than with the "ultimate why." As William James has said: "Pragmatism is the attitude of looking away from first things, principles, categories, supposed necessities; and of looking forward toward last things, fruits, consequences, facts." As another writer has said: "Modern psychology is essentially prismatic in its treatment of the subject of the mind in giving to metaphysics the old arguments and disputes regarding the ultimate nature of mind, it bends all its energies upon discovering the laws of mental activities and states, and developing methods whereby the mind may be trained to perform better and more work, to conserve its energies, to concentrate its forces. To modern psychology the mind is something to be used, not merely something about which to postulate and theorize. While the metaphysicians deplore this tendency, the practical people of the world rejoice."

Mind Mastery vs. Mind Slavery
But, you may say, what do you mean by "The Master Mind?" What is the difference between a Master Mind and any other form of Mind? Simply this, good readers, that the Master Mind is consciously, deliberately, and voluntarily built up, cultivated, developed, and

9

used; whereas the ordinary mind is usually unconsciously built up, cultivated, and developed, without voluntary effort on its own part, but solely by the force and power of impressions from the outside world, and is usually employed and used with little or no conscious direction by its own will. In short, the ordinary mind is a mere creature of circumstances, driven hither and thither by the winds of outside forces, and lacking the guidance of the hand on the wheel, and being without the compass of knowledge; while the Master Mind proceeds in the true course mapped out by Intelligence, and determined by will—with sails set so as to catch the best breeze from the outside world, and steered by the master-hand at the wheel, under the direction of the compass of intelligence. The ordinary mind is like a dumb, driven animal, while the Master Mind is like the strong-willed, intelligent, masterful Man.

The average man is a very slave to his thoughts and feelings. A stream of thought and feeling flows through him, moving him hither and thither with little or no voluntary choice on his own part. Even those men who have attained a certain degree of mental mastery do but little more than to feebly steer their mental bark by the rudder of a wobbling will—they do not realize that Mastery is possible to them. Even a

well known writer has said: ''We do not voluntarily create our thinking. It takes place in
us. We are more or less passive recipients. We
cannot change the nature of a thought; but we
can, as it were, guide the ship by a moving of
the helm.'' It would be truer to say that we can
deliberately and voluntarily select and choose
the particular wind which is to force our mental
boat forward or, changing the figure, to choose
and select the particular stream of thought and
feeling which is to be allowed to flow through
our mind.

There are three general conditions of human
mentality, viz.: (1) Mental Slavery, in which the
mind is the slave and servant of outside forces
and influences; (2) Partial Freedom, in which
the mind is largely controlled by outside influences, while at the same time a limited amount
of voluntary control and direction has been
acquired; and

(3) Mental Mastery, in which the mental faculties, and emotional organism have been brought
under the control of the will and judgment, and
the individual is a master of, and not a slave
to, environment and circumstances. The great
masses of persons are in the first or the above
named classes; a comparatively small number
have passed into the second class; while a still

smaller number have passed into the third class, and have become the Master Minds of their time and place.

A talented writer has said along these lines: "We moderns are unaccustomed to the mastery over our inner thoughts and feelings. That a man should be a prey to any thought that chances to take possession of his mind, is commonly among us assumed as unavoidable. It may be a matter of regret that he should be kept awake all night from anxiety as to the issue of a lawsuit on the morrow, and that he should have the power of determining whether he be kept awake or not seems an extravagant demand. The image of an impending calamity is no doubt odious, but its very odiousness (we say) makes it haunt the mind all the more pertinaciously, and it is useless to expel it. Yet this is an absurd position for man, the heir of all the ages, to be in: lag-ridden by the flimsy creatures of his own brain. If a pebble in our boot torments us, we expel it. We take off the boot and shake it out. And once the matter is fairly understood, it is just as easy to expel an intruding and obnoxious thought from the mind. About this there ought to be no mistake, no two opinions. The thing is obvious, clear and unmistakable. It should be as easy to expel an obnoxious thought from the mind as to shake a stone out of your shoe; and until a man can do that, it is just nonsense to talk about his ascendancy over nature, and all the rest of it. He is a mere slave, and a prey to the bat-winged phantoms that flit through the corridors of his own brain. Yet the weary and careworn faces that we meet by thousands, even among the affluent classes of civilization, testify only too clearly how seldom this mastery is obtained. How rare indeed to find a man! How common rather to discover a creature hounded on by tyrant thoughts (or cares, or desires), cowering, wincing under the lash—or perchance priding himself to run merrily to a driver that rattles the reins and persuades him that he is free—whom he cannot converse with in careless tete-a-tete because that alien presence is always there, on the watch.

"It is one of the prominent doctrines of some of the oriental schools of practical psychology that the power of expelling thoughts, or if need be, killing them dead on the spot, must be attained. Naturally the art requires practice, but like other arts, when once acquired there is no mystery or difficulty about it. It is worth practice. It may be fairly said that life only begins when this art has been acquired. For obviously when, instead of being ruled by individual thoughts, the whole flock of them in their immense multitude and variety and capacity is ours to direct and dispatch and employ where we list, life becomes a thing so vast and grand, compared to what it was before, that its former condition may well appear almost ante-natal. If you can kill a thought dead, for the time being, you can do anything else with it that you please. And therefore it is that this power is so valuable. And it not only frees a man from mental torment (which is nine-tenths at least of the torment of life), but it gives him a concentrated power of handling mental work absolutely unknown to him before. The two are co-relative to each other.

"While at work your thought is to he absolutely concentrated upon and in it, undistracted by anything whatever irrelevant to the matter in hand—pounding away like a great engine, with giant power and perfect economy—no wear and tear or friction, or dislocation of parts owing to the working of different forces at the same time. Then when the work is finished, if there is no more occasion for the use of the machine, it must stop equally, absolutely—stop entirely—no worrying (as if a parcel of boys were allowed to play their devilments with a locomotive as soon as it was in the shed)—and the man must retire into that region of his consciousness where his true self dwells.

"I say that the power of the thought-machine is enormously increased by this faculty of letting it alone on the one hand, and of using it singly and with concentration on the other. It becomes a true tool, which a master-workman lays down when done with, but which only a bungler carries about with him all the time to show that he is the possessor of it. Then on and beyond the work turned out by the tool itself is the knowledge that comes to us apart from its use; when the noise of the workshop is over, and mallet and plane laid aside—the faint sounds coming through the open window from the valley and the far seashore; the dim fringe of diviner knowledge which begins to grow, poor thing, as soon as the eternal click-clack of thought is over—the extraordinary intuitions, perceptions, which though partaking in some degree of the character of the thought, spring from entirely different conditions, and are the forerunners of a changed consciousness.

"The subjection of thought is closely related to the subjection of desire, and has consequently its specially moral as well as its specially intellectual relation to the question in hand. Ninetenths of the scattered or sporadic thought with which the mind usually occupies itself when not concentrated on any definite work, is what may be called self-thought—thought of a kind which dwells on and exaggerates the sense of self. This is hardly realized in its full degree till the effort is made to suppress it; and one of the most excellent results of such an effort is that with the stilling of all the phantoms which hover around the lower self, one's relations to others, to one's friends, to the world at large, and one's perceptions of all that is concerned in these relations, come out into a purity and distinctness unknown before. Obviously, when the mind is full of little desires and fears which concern the local self, and is clouded over by the thought images which such desires and fears evoke, it is impossible that it should see and understand the greater facts beyond, and its own relation to them. But with the subsiding of the former, the great vision begins to dawn; and a man never feels less alone than when he has ceased to think whether he is alone or not."

From the above the reader may get a general idea of what we mean when we speak of the Master Mind. But, as we proceed with the unfoldment of the general idea upon which this book is based, the reader will catch the spirit of the idea in a way impossible for him now when the subject has been presented to him merely in its general aspects. There are so many angles of viewpoint, and so many varied applications of the general principle involved, that it is necessary for the careful student of the subject to understand the many details of the presentation before he can expect to "catch the spirit of it," at least to the extent of being able to put into actual practice the working method which will be presented for his consideration in this book. But, it may be safely stated that any one of average intelligence, with ordinary study and practice, may master these principles and methods of application to such an extent that he will know for himself, by actual results obtained, that he is no longer a Mental Slave but has developed into a Mental Master.

The individual of the Master Mind is able to so control his powers of attention and concentration that he will be able to choose and select exactly the kind of thoughts and ideas which he requires in his business of life and effort. Moreover, he will be able to manifest these thoughts and ideas into effective and efficient action and expression, so as to obtain precisely the kind of results desired by him. Moreover, he will be able to govern, select, control, and choose the character and quality of his thoughts and ideas, but also to manifest the same power regarding his emotions and feelings, his tastes and "likes." And this last is very important, for, as we shall see presently, most of our thoughts and ideas come to us in response to our feelings, desires, and likes.

Not only this, but the individual of the Master Mind is able to set to work intelligently, and under full control, those marvelous faculties which operate on the subconscious planes of mind, and which are able and willing to perform much of our mental work for us below the surface of ordinary consciousness, and thus leave free for other tasks the faculties ordinarily employed in the thinking processes. It is believed by the best authorities on the subject that fully eighty-five percent of our mental activities are performed on planes under the surface of our ordinary consciousness. This being so, it is seen at once that one who is able to control and master these subconscious metal activities will and must be capable of results impossible to those who allow their subconscious mentality to wander about like horses in a pasture, or else rush like runaway horses in whatever direction they like and thus wreck the chariot rather than reaching the goal of the ambitious.

In short, the individual of the Master Mind is indeed a MASTER of his mental machinery, and is able to turn out a mental product of the highest quality and degree of efficiency. And, thus being the Master of himself, he becomes the Master of much in the outside world. To the

Master Mind, even circumstances seem to come under conscious control and management; and other men and women seem to be ready to accept direction and control from such a masterful mentality. The Master Mind creates a world for itself, in which it dwells supreme, and to which it attracts and draws that which is conducive to its welfare and happiness, its success and achievement.

You are invited to become a Master Mind. Will you accept the invitation? If so, you will carefully study the principles herein explained, and apply the methods herein set forth and described.

The Mind Master

The idea of "mastery" inevitably carries with it the notion of dominion, power, or supremacy exercised by some person or thing which is regarded as the "master." The spirit and essence of the term ''master'' is that of ''governor, ruler, director, leader, manager, or controller.'' In short, the essential meaning of the two terms, "master" and "mastery," respectively, is bound up with the idea of "government." To "govern" anything, the governing authority regulates, directs, restrains, manages, entourages, and exercises general control and direction.

In all forms of government there is to be found a certain central point of authority—a certain central power which is sovereign within its own realm, and which has the authority to promulgate commands and the authority to enforce them. Whether the government is that exercised by the chief of a savage tribe, who gains and holds his position by means of physical strength; whether it be that of the monarch of a kingdom, who gains and holds his position by hereditary rights; or whether it be that of the president of a republic, who gains and holds his position by the will of the people; the central authority is vested in some one particular individual. And, descending in the scale, we find the same principle in operation and force in the government of a public meeting, a school room, a workshop, or an office. In short, wherever there is government, there must be a central governing authority—a Master.

The above general principle being recognized, the reasoning mind at once applies it to the question of the operation and government of the mental powers and faculties. If the mind is held to be "governed" at all, or to be capable of "government" (and who can doubt this?), then there must be some central governing authority—some Mind Master whose authority, when exercised, is recognized and obeyed by the other mental units, powers, faculties, or forces. This being so, the reasoning investigator then naturally proceeds to the discovery of this Mind Master. Let us play the part of this reasoning investigator, and proceed with him to the discovery of the Mind Master—the central point of authority and power in the kingdom of mind.

Some psychologists would have us believe that the intellectual faculties are the governing powers of the mind. But it will take but little thought to inform us that in many cases the intellectual powers are not the masterful forces in the mental activities of the individual; for in many cases the feelings, desires, and emotional factors of the person run away with his reason, and not only cause him to do things which his reason tells him that he should not do, but also so influence his reason that his "reasons" are usually merely excuses to his actions performed in response to his feelings and emotions.

Other psychologists would have us believe that the desires, feelings, and emotions of the individual are his mental masters; and in many cases it would appear that this is true, for many persons allow their feelings, emotions, and passions to govern them almost entirely, all else being subordinated to these. But when we begin to examine closely into the matter we find that in the case of certain individuals there is a greater or less subordination of the feelings and emotions to the dictates of reason; and in the case of persons of excellent self-control the reason would appear to be higher in authority than the feelings. And in the case of recognized Mental Masters, it is even found that the very feelings, passions, and emotions are so obedient to higher mental authority that in many cases they may actually be transformed and transmuted into other forms of feeling and emotion in response to the orders or commands of the central authority.

The reasoning investigator usually discovers
that the Mind Master is not to be found in the
respective realms of the first two of the three
great divisions of the mental kingdom, i.e.,
in the division of Thought, or that of Feeling,
respectively. The investigator then turns to the
third great division of the mental kingdom,
i.e., that of Will, in his search for the sovereign
power. And at first, it would appear that here, in
the region of the Will, he had found the object
of his search; and that the Will must be ac-
claimed the master. But when the matter is gone
into a little deeper, the investigator discovers
that not in Will itself, but in a Something lying at the very center of Will, is to be found the
Mind Master.

While it is seen that the Will is higher in power
and authority than either Thought or Feeling,
yet it is also seen by the careful investigator
that in most cases the Will is controlled and
brought into activity by the Feelings; and that in
other cases, it is started into action by the result
of Thought or intellectual effort. This being so,
the Will cannot be considered as being always
the Mind Master. And, discovering this, the
investigator at first begins to feel discouraged,
and to imagine that he is but traveling around a
circle; in fact, many thinkers would have us believe that the mental processes work around in

a circle, and that like a ring the process has no point of beginning or point of ending. But those who have persisted in the search have been rewarded by a higher discovery. They have found that while many persons are impelled to will by reason of their feelings and emotions; and others by reason of their thoughts; there is a third class of individuals—a smaller class to be sure—who seem to be masters of the will-activity, and who, standing in the position of a judge and sovereign power, first carefully weigh the merits of both feelings and thoughts, and then decide to exercise the will-power in a certain determined direction, and then actually do exert that power. This last class of individuals may be said to really will to will by the exercise of some higher authority found within themselves. These men are the real Master Minds. Let us seek to discover the secret of their power.

The Central Authority
There is in the mental realm of every individual a certain Something which occupies the position of Central Authority, Power, and Control over the entire mental kingdom of that person. In many cases —in most cases, we regret to say—this Something seems to be asleep, and the kingdom is allowed to run itself, "higgledy-piggledy," automatically and like a piece of senseless machinery, or else under the control

of outside mentalities and personalities. In other cases—in many cases, in fact—this Central Authority has partially awakened, and consequently exerts at least a measure of its authority over its kingdom, but at the same time fails to realize its full powers or to exert its full authority; it acts like a man only half awakened from his sleep, and still in a state of partial doze.

Rising in the scale we find cases of still greater degree of "awakening," until finally we discover the third great class of individuals—a very small class, alas!—in whom the Central Authority has become almost or quite fully awake; and in whom this Mind Master has taken active control of his kingdom, and has begun to assert his authority and power over it. This first class is composed of the masses of the people; the second class is composed of those who occupy positions and places of more or less authority and power in the world's affairs; and the third class is composed of those exceptional individuals who are the natural rulers of the destiny of the race, and directors of its activities—the real Master Minds.

There is only one way of aiding the investigator to discover this Something—this Central Authority—this Mind Master. That one way consists of directing the investigator to turn his perception inward, and to take stock of his numerous mental faculties, powers, activities, and bits of mechanism, and to then set aside as merely incidental and subordinate all that appears to be so. When all these have been set aside in the process of elimination, then there will be found a Something which is left after the process, and which absolutely refuses to be set aside as merely incidental and subordinate—and that Something is then perceived to be the Central Authority, or Mind Master, even though it be half-asleep, and unconscious of its great powers. But for that matter, no Mind Master which is deeply wrapped in slumber will ever discover itself, for it must have been at least partially awakened in order (1) to have thought of the matter at all, or to be capable of thought on the subject; and (2) to have to power of attention and application necessary to pursue the investigation. So, good reader, if you have the desire to find the Mind Master (which is Yourself), it is a sign that you have at least partially awakened; and if you have the determination to pursue the search, it is a sign that you are still further awakened. So you are justified in feeling the courage and the certainty of attainment necessary for the successful termination of the search for the Mind Master—the Something within yourself.

You, the person now reading these words—
YOU, yourself—are now asked to make this
search of your mental kingdom, this search
which has for its aim the discovery of the
Something Within yourself which is the Mind
Master, and which, when fully aroused into
conscious power and activity, makes you a
Master Mind. The writer will stand by your side
during this search, and will point out to you
at each stage of the search the essential points
thereof. You will not be asked to accept any
metaphysical theories, or religious dogmas: the
search will be confined to strictly psychological
fields, and will proceed along strictly scientific
lines. You will not be asked to accept the authority of anyone else in the matter: your own
consciousness will be the court of last appeal in
the case.

The Mental Analysis

Let us begin with your sensations, or report of
your senses. You are constantly receiving reports of one or more of your five senses, viz.,
the respective senses of touch, taste, smell,
sight, and hearing. All these reports are in the
form and nature of impressions received from
the outside world. All that we know of the
outside world is made known to us by means of
these impressions received through the senses.

A writer has said: "The senses are the means by which the mind obtains its knowledge of the outside world. Shut out from all direct communication with the outer world, it knows, and can know, nothing of what exists or is passing there, except what comes to it through the senses. Its knowledge of what is external to itself is therefore dependent upon the number, state and condition of the sensory organs." But, important as are the five senses and their mechanism, we need but a little thought to convince us that we do not find here the essential fact and power of mind, but rather merely incidental and subordinate powers. We can easily prove this to ourselves in many ways. For instance, we may shut out or shut off the channel of communication of any or all of the channels of the senses, and still be conscious of our own mental existence. Or, we may use the will, through the power of attention, and thus determine which of the many sets of sense impressions seeking admission to our consciousness we shall really receive and entertain in consciousness. We may thus choose between many sounds, or many sights, and deliberately shut out the others. If the sense impressions were the Masters, we could not do this; and so long as we are able to do this, we must look for the Master higher up in the scale.

Moreover, in all of our experience with these

sense impressions, we never lose sight of the fact that they are but incidental facts of our mental existence, and that there is a Something Within which is really the Subject of these sense reports—a Something to which these reports are presented, and which receives them. In short, there is always the Something which knows or experiences these sensations. We recognize and express this fact when we say "I feel; I see; I hear," etc. There is always the thing- sensed, then the process of sensing, and finally the Something which experiences the sensation. This Something we speak of as "I." The "I" is always the subject which experiences the sense reports—the Something to whom the messages are presented. And as this Something is capable of either accepting or rejecting, or selecting and controlling, these messages or reports, then the latter cannot be regarded as the Mind Master.

In the same way, we next proceed to the consideration of the Emotional phases of our mentality. In this great realm of the mind we may, at least for the purposes of the present inquiry, include all those mental experiences that come under the respective head of "feelings," "passions," "desires," etc. These seem a little closer to us than did the sensations. This because the sensations came from outside of ourselves, while the emotions and feelings seem to come from within a part of ourselves. The emotional part of our nature is very powerful, so powerful, indeed, that it often seems to rule the entire being of the individual. But a little careful examination will convince us that we may, by the use of the will, not only refuse to obey our emotional urges and demands, but may even destroy them, or replace them with others.

If our emotions were really Masters, we would be bound to act upon them at ali times, and upon all occasions, for there would be nothing in us to say Nay! to them. But no one outside of the most primitive and elemental individuals would permit any such rule on the part of the emotional nature, even the less advanced of the race are able to at least partially control and manage the emotional part of their mental nature; and the advanced individuals have acquired the power of frequently deliberately setting aside the dictates of the emotions, and of asserting the power of control over them. So, here too, we see that the Master must be looked for higher up in the scale.

As in the case of the sensations, here too, in the case of the emotions we discover the presence of that Something Within which is the Subject of the emotions—the Something to which the emotions report, and from whom they demand action. Here again we find this "I" occupying a higher seat, and having the reports and demands of the subordinate faculties made upon it. And, mark you this, that in spite of the constant change in the emotional stream of feeling, this "I" always remains the same. Just as in the case of the sensations, the "I" occupies the position of a spectator to whom are presented the sense experiences, so in the case of the emotions the "I" occupies the position of the Something which experiences the ever changing "feeling" of the emotional nature. In both cases there seems to be this constant Something, past which flows the respective streams of Sensations and Emotions. And this Something also has the power to direct and change the course of these streams, if it will but exert its Will Power.

Next we consider the great realm of Thought. Here, too, we find a constant stream of thoughts flowing past the Something—the "I"—which is practically the spectator of the flowing stream; and which also has the power of directing and controlling the stream. While it is true that the individuals of primitive natures are almost passive spectators of the streams of their thoughts, and exercise little or no control over them, it is an unquestioned fact that other individuals who have cultivated their Will Power are able to turn their attention to this kind of thoughts, or that kind, and thus control and determine just what kind of thoughts they shall think. Every student performs this feat of control and mastery when he voluntarily directs his attention to some particular study which he desires to master. In fact, all "voluntary attention" is performed by the exercise of this power of the will, exerted by this Something Within which we call "I," and which thus proves itself to be the Master of Thoughts.

The individual who has trained his mind to obey his will, is able to direct his thought processes just as he directs his feet, or his hands, or his body, or just as he guides and manages his team or horses or his motor car. This being so, we cannot consider our Thought processes or faculties as the Mind Master, but must look for the latter in something still higher in authority.

There seems to be but one other region of the mind in which to search for our Mind Master, or Central Authority. You naturally say here "He means The Will." But is it merely the Will? Stop a moment and consider. If the Will, in itself, is the Mind Master, why is it that the Will, in the case of so many persons, allows itself to be controlled and called into action by ordinary feelings, desires, emotions, or passions, or on the other hand is called into action by the most trifling passing thought or idea? In such cases it would appear that the Will is really the obedient "easy" servant, rather than the Master, does it not.

That the machinery of the Will is the mechanism of control and action, is undoubted; but what is it that controls and directs the Will in the cases of individuals of strong Will Power? In such cases it would seem that not only must the Will be strong, but that there must be some stronger Something which is able to control, direct, and apply the power of the Will. In moments in which you have exerted your Will Power, did you identify yourself with your Will, or did you feel that your Will was an instrument of power "belonging to" you, and being operated by you. Were you not at such moments aware of feeling an overwhelming consciousness of the existence of your self, or "I," at the center of your mental being? and of feeling that, at least for the time, this "I" was the Master of all the rest of your mental equipment? We think that you will agree to this statement, if you will carefully live over again the experiences of such moments, and in imagination and memory re-enact the experience.

All mental analysis brings the individual to the realization that at the very center of his mental being there abides and dwells a Something—and he always calls this "I"— which is the permanent element of his being. While his sensations, his feelings, his emotions, his tastes, his thoughts, his beliefs, his ideas, and even his ideals have changed from time to time, he knows to a certainty that this "I" has been permanent, and that it is the same old "I" that has always been present during his entire life, from his earliest days. He knows that although his emotional nature, and general mental physical character may have undergone an almost total transformation and change, yet this "I" has never been really changed at all, but has ever remained "the same old I." It is as if this "I" was an individual who had worn many successive coats, or shoes, or hats, but always remained the same individual. The consciousness of every individual must always so report to him, when the answer is demanded of it.

And, moreover, while the individual may and does change his sensations, his feelings, his tastes, his passions, his emotions, and his whole general character in some cases, he is never able to change in the slightest degree this Something Within which he calls "I." He can never run away from this "I," nor can he ever move it from its position. He can never lift his "I" by means of his mental bootstraps; nor can his personal shadow run away from this "I" of his individuality. He may set apart for consideration each and every one of his mental experiences, his sensations, his thoughts, his feelings, his ideas, and all the rest; but he can never set off from himself this "I" for such inspection. He can know this "I" only as his self, that Something Within at the very center of his consciousness.

A writer has said of this Something Within, which we call "I": "We are conscious of something closer to the center than anything else, and differing from the other forms in being the only form of consciousness to which we are not passive. This Something is in the normal consciousness of each of you, yet it is never a part of sensation, nor emotion, but on the contrary is capable of dominating both.

Sensations originate outside and inside of the body; Emotions originate inside of the body. But this Something is deeper than either, and they are both objective to it. We cannot classify it with anything else. We cannot describe it in terms of any other form of consciousness. We cannot separate ourselves from it. We cannot stand off and examine it. We cannot modify it by anything else. It, itself, modifies everything within its scope. Other forms of conscious-

35

ness are objective in their relation to it, but it is never objective to them. There is nothing in our consciousness deeper. It underlies and over-lies and permeates all other forms, and, more-over,—what is of immeasurably greater impor-tance,—it can, if need be, create them."

Another writer has said: "The 'I' is the Thinker, the Knower, the Feeler, the Actor. Its states of consciousness are constantly changing—differ-ent today from those of yesterday, and different tomorrow from those of today—but the 'I,' it-self, is always the name. Just what this 'I' is, we cannot tell. This riddle has never been solved by the reason of man. So subtle is its essence that it is almost impossible to think of it as a something apart from its mental states. All that can be said of it is that it is. Its only report of it-self is 'I Am.' You cannot examine the 'I' by the 'I.' You must have an object for your subject; and if you make the 'I' your object, you have no subject left to examine it. Place the 'I' under the mental microscope to examine it, and lo! you have nothing to look through the glass —there is no 'I' at the eye-piece of the microscope to examine it. The 'I' cannot be at both ends of the glass at the same time. Here, at last, you have found an Ultimate Something which defies all analysis, refinement, or separation."

This Something Within—this "I"—is that entity which in philosophy and metaphysics has been called "The Ego"; but such name does nothing in the way of defining it. You need not stop to speculate over "just what" the Ego is, for you will never learn this. All that you can know is that it IS—and you know this from the ultimate report of your own consciousness, and in no other way, for nothing outside of yourself can make you know this otherwise.

This Ego is the Mind Master—the Central Authority of your Mind. It is this that is able to master, control, manage, rule, regulate and direct all of your mental faculties, energies, powers, forces, and mechanism. It is this Ego, when fully awakened into activity, which constitutes the essence of the Master Mind.

Your task is not to try to learn "just what" the Ego is, for as has been said, you will never know this. Your task is to strive to awaken it into active consciousness, so that it may realize its power and begin to employ it. You can awaken it by the proper mental attitude toward it—by the conscious realization of its presence and power. And you can gradually cause it to realize its power, and to use the same, by means of exercises calling into play that power. This is what Will Power really means. Your Will is strong already—it does not need strengthening; what is needed is that you urge your Ego into realizing that it can use your Will Power, and to teach it to use the same by means of the right kind of exercises. You must learn to gradually awaken the half-asleep Giant, and set it to work in its own natural field of endeavor and activity. In this book the way will be pointed out to you so that you may do this; but you will have to actively DO the thing, after being shown how He who will, carefully consider the above statements of truth, and will make them apart of his mental armament, will have grasped the secret of the Master Mind.

The Slave Will and the Master Will

All deep students of psychology discover that the Will is the innermost, garment of the Ego—the mental sheath which lies beneath all the others, and which clings closely to the substance of the Ego, so closely that it can scarcely be distinguished from its wearer. And so, the race has become accustomed to identifying the Will with the Ego. For instance, we speak of a "weak will," or a "strong will," a "vacillating will," or a "persistent, determined will"; when we really mean to indicate the different degrees of the activity and expression of the Ego itself.

Perhaps you will get more clearly this conception of the Ego behind the Will, if we continue our illustration of the Ego as sleeping in the cast of the great masses of the race, half-awake in the smaller portion of the race, and wide-awake in the elect few who may be called the Master Minds. While this illustration is of course figurative, it is based upon the actual facts of the case before us, and, moreover, comes so closely to the real manifestations of the Ego that it may he used in almost a literal sense.

The sleeping Ego is like a person wrapped in slumber, who is almost unconscious, but who will "turn over," or "move over" at the command of the bedfellow. In some cases the degree of waking-consciousness is somewhat higher, as in the case of the child who, half roused from slumber, will do what it is told by its parent, but without clearly realizing just what it is doing. This illustration may be carried even still further, and the sleeping Ego compared to the somnambulist, or "sleep-walker," who "goes through the motions" of performing many tasks and actions, but who is but very dimly conscious (or practically unconscious) of just what he is doing or how he is doing it.

The masses of the race, in whom the Ego is dwelling in this condition, are really little more than automatons. Their wills are called into activity by every passing desire, their passions and desires are uncontrolled, and their thought-processes are the result of suggestions made by others but which they accept and then fondly imagine they have thought the thing for themselves. They are like the wind-harps upon which the winds of the passing breeze blow, and from which the responsive sounds are produced. It is a fact known to careful students of psychology that in the case of the masses of the race the mental processes, and the will activity, are practically those of an automaton, or psychical machine, there being little or no voluntary effort exerted or voluntary choice or decision made.

The wills of such persons are Slave Wills, subject to the influence, control, and direction of others; although their owners may fondly imagine that they are sound thinkers and possessed of powerful wills. The will processes of such persons are almost entirely what are known as "reflex" activities, requiring the employment of but little powers of judgment and little or no exercise of voluntary control. Do you realize just what this means? Probably not; so you are asked to consider what ''reflex'' activity really is.

The following quotation from a leading psychologist will throw some light on the matter for you. This writer says: "Reflex nervous action is the result of that power resident in nervous ganglia, which often unconsciously causes many muscular and vital movements. The spinal cord is largely made up of such masses of nervous matter, which have sometimes been called 'little brains.' If one were to prick the foot of a sleeper, the sensory nerve at that point would report the fact to one of the lower spinal nerve masses. This ganglion, without waiting to hear from the brain, would issue a command to the motor nerve, and the foot would be immediately withdrawn. Unless the thrust were severe, the sleeper would not awake, nor would he be conscious of pain or of the movement of his foot. This nervous action is called 'reflex,' because, when the sensory nerve conveys an impulse to the ganglion, this impulse is at once, and without the action of the mind, reflected back by a motor nerve. Thus the mind is not only saved the trouble of attending to every little movement, but much time is gained. After the child has learned the difficult art of balancing himself on his feet, walking becomes largely a reflex act. At first, the child must center his whole attention on movements to balance the body. The man can think out the most complex problems while walking, because the reflex nervous centers are superintending the balancing process.

"Few men remember which end of the collar they button on first, or which shoe they put on first, yet the reflex nerve center, if left to itself, has an invariable order in executing these movements. Some vertebrates have much more reflex power than man. The spinal cord in such animals keeps its vitality for a long time after decapitation, and the nerve masses in the cord have the power to set the motor nerves in action, causing muscular contraction. For this reason a decapitated snake will squirm around in a lively manner if its tail is struck. The reason why fowls often flutter so violently after the fatal stroke is because they are thrown roughly down. The sensory nerves report the bruise or jar to a reflex center, which agitates the motor nerves controlling the muscles which would ordinarily move them out of a harmless way. If beheaded fowls are laid carefully on straw or some soft substance, they will scarcely move. But if they should be kicked a moment or two later, they will frequently jump around in a lively manner. If acid is placed on the side of a decapitated frog, the animal will, by reflex action, bring its foot to the spot and try to brush the drop away. Man also has something of this reflex power after death. The pectoral muscle of a be-headed French criminal was pinched, and the right hand was raised to the spot as if to remove the cause of the injury."

Some may object that we are making too strong a statement when we say that the mental activity of the great masses of people are practically akin to the "reflex" actions above described. People "think" about what they do, before doing it, these objectors say. Of course "people think"; or, rather, they "think that they think"; but in reality the process of their "thinking" is almost reflex, that is to say it is automatic and mechanical rather than deliberate and controlled by will and judgment. Their thought is usually based upon some suggested premise—some so-called fact accepted through suggestion from others and without verification or duo consideration. Their accepted "facts" are usually found to be those which agree with their likes, feelings, or prejudices, rather than which are based upon careful and unprejudiced investigation. If the facts do not agree with these prejudices and wishes, then "so much the worse for the facts," and the latter are discarded, and eliminated from the so-called "thinking."

And the process of reasoning of these people is likewise lop-sided and unsound in principle. Their so-called "reasons" are but excuses or explanations evolved to justify their decision or action, both of the latter being really based upon the desires, wishes, likes, or prejudices of the person, rather than upon his cool and deliberate judgment. But, you may say, you are now speaking of the person's thoughts, while a moment ago you wore speaking of his will; what do you mean by this? Simply this, good reader, that "thoughts take form in action," and all will actions are based upon thoughts or feelings. Therefore if the person's thoughts are "reflex," then his will action is likewise. We have spoken of the reflex character of the man's actions which were based upon his "thoughts," let us now examine his actions based upon his "feelings." We will soon discover that these too are practically reflex.

It is held by the best psychologists that practically all voluntary acts of will result from the power of desire. This, of course, includes actions resulting from fear, or repulsion, both of which are but negative phases of desire (being the desire "not to experience"). But this does not imply, by any means, that all desires result in will action. On the contrary, in the person of self-control, the greater portion of his desires are inhibited, restrained, controlled, or even killed. The rule is this: The Greater the degree of the will-power of the individual, the greater is his degree of control over his desires. And, as we have seen that the degree of will-power is the degree of the "wakefulness" of the Ego, it follows that the greater the wakefulness of the Ego, the greater the degree of its control over the desires found within its mental realm. As the Ego of most persons is in a state or more or less asleep, it follows that we should expect to find among such people but a slight degree of control of desire, and consequently of their actions resulting from desire; and investigation discloses precisely this kind or result.

The animal, the young child, and the undeveloped man is impelled to act freely upon each and every desire or feeling that manifests within his mental being; he is restrained from such action only by fear of consequences. It is related of certain savage tribes that it is unwise to issue them several days' rations when starting on a journey, because they will sit down and eat the entire ration at one meal, being unable to resist the inclination, and being unable to control the appetite of the moment in the interest of the certain hunger of tomorrow, and the next day, and the day after. We smile at this, but how many of us are quite as foolish when we sacrifice the success of tomorrow and the next day upon the altar of the satisfaction of the desires of the present moment. The desire-action of the Slave Will is almost purely reflex and under no voluntary control; while that of the Master Will is under great voluntary control and direction. We shall see more of this when we reach the place in this book in which the subject of Desire is considered in detail.

Some philosophers have sought to convince us that Man is never more than an automaton—a creature of reflex activities—having no freedom of choice, will, and action. And so strong do they make their one side of the case, that many have accepted their reasoning. But the truth is grasped only when we consider the other side of the ease; then the real truth is seen to rest between the two extremes. It is seen to be true that in the cases of the masses of the race—the persons of the Slave Will— there is little or no real freedom of action, but rather there is an almost automatic response of will-action to desire-motive. But, on the other hand, in the case of the advanced few of the race, the true individuals—the persons of the Master Will—there is secured the longed for freedom of action, by means of the control of the desire- motives. In fact, this control is one of the leading characteristics of the Master Mind.

_ M.A
_ Padmasambhava
_ Dumont

A leading; authority has well said: "All persons agree that there is no such thing as unrestrained freedom of action. Every human being is, from the cradle to the grave, subject to external restraint. If a man declares that he is free to go without food, air, and sleep, and tries to act accordingly, consequences will soon deprive him of that liberty. The circle of freedom is much smaller than is sometimes thought; the fish is never free to become an eagle. Human freedom may be likened to a vessel sailing up a river. Her course must be kept rigidly within the banks; she cannot sail on the dry land; but by tacking, she can make headway up the stream in the teeth of the wind, and she can stop either at this town or at that. The popular belief is correct, that the sphere of freedom is sufficiently wide to allow a man scope enough to keep him busy for several lifetimes.

"Freedom consists in being able to choose between two or more alternative courses of action. A stone is limited to one course and is subject to an unvarying law of gravity. Exclude the power of choice, will all freedom is gone. If we have the power of alternative choice, we are within certain limits free. These limits vary. If I am educated so that I know how to do several different things in the higher walks of life, I can choose any of these things. If I am ignorant and can perform only cruder tasks, my capacity for choice is excluded from higher hues of action. Some deny that human beings have any more freedom than a stone."

The average man will indignantly deny that his freedom of will action is in any way affected or restricted by outside or inside influences. He says triumphantly: "I can act as I wish," think- ing that he has answered the argument against free will. But here is the point: he can act only as he wishes; and if his wishes are controlled or determined in any way, then so are his actions controlled and determined. And as his "wishes" are but forms of his desires, then unless he con- trols his desires he does not control his wishes, but is controlled by them. And as the average man has not acquired a strong control of his desires, he is lacking to that extent in his freedom of will action. And right here is the main distinction between the man of the Slave Will mid the man of the Master Will.

The Slave Will obeys the orders of its desires, feelings, and other "wishes," the latter coming from Lord-knows-where into his mental field. Such a man is not free, in the true sense of the word. He is a slave to his wishes, his feelings, his desires, his passions—and he has no control, over the thoughts and ideas which feed these desires, and which often actually create them. The Master Will not only refuses to he controlled by the intruding desires, if these are deemed against his best interests, but he actually controls them—this last by controlling the ideas and thoughts which serve to feed and nourish these desires, and which in many cases also have actually created them.

A leading authority speaking upon the subject of this control of desire (and consequently of will action) by means of the control of the power of thought, ideas, through attention, has given the world the following remarkably strong, clear, and true statement of the case; you are advised to carefully read and consider the same. The authority in question says:

"At the threshold of each higher act of will stands desire. All feeling tends to excite desire. Sometimes desire gives rise to intense feeling. In one aspect, desire is feeling; in another, desire is will or an active tension which passes imperceptibly into will. In desire, properly so called, there must be a definite idea. If a person says 'I desire,' the question very naturally is, 'What?' Unless there is a definite answer to the question, desire is not the name to apply to that mental state. There are always at least two alternatives in any line of conduct. When we face an orchestra, we have the choice of listening to it as a whole, or of selecting some one instrument, such as the first violin, and paying attention to it. In looking at a landscape, we choose certain elements for close inspection. Our world is, therefore, very much what we choose to pay attention to. If we visit the tropics and choose to heed nothing but the venomous animals, the land will be chiefly one of snakes and centipedes; if we look principally at the birds and flowers, it will be to us largely a clime of song and perfume.

"Ideas detained in consciousness tend to fan the flame of feeling; these ideas may be dismissed and others summoned to repress the flame of feeling. In the higher type of action, the will can go out only in the direction of an idea. Every idea which becomes an object of desire is a motive. It is true that the will tends to go out in the direction of the greatest motive, that is, toward the object which seems the most desirable; but the will, through voluntary attention, puts energy into a motive idea and thus makes it strong. It is impossible to center the attention long on an idea without developing positive or negative interest, attraction or repulsion. Thus does the will develop motives. We may state it as a law that the will determines which motives shall become the strongest, by determining which ideas shall occupy the field of consciousness.

"We have seen that emotion and desire arise in the presence of ideas, and that the will has influence in detaining or in banishing a given idea. If one idea is kept before the mind, a desire and a strong motive may gather around that idea. If another idea is called in, the power of the first idea will decline. The more Macbeth and his wife held before themselves the idea of the fame and power which the throne would confer upon them, the stronger became the desire to kill the king, until finally it grew too strong to be mastered. They were, however, responsible for nursing the desire; had they resolutely thought of something else, that desire would have been weakened. The person who feeds a bad desire with the fitting ideas will find that some day the desire will master his will.

"In the capacity for attention we have the way to the freedom of the will. Voluntary attention makes the motive. The motive does not make the attention. Hence the motive is a product of the will. If I withdraw my attention from a motive idea, it loses vigor, like a plant deprived of air and moisture. By sheer force of will, many a one has withdrawn his attention from certain temptations, centered it elsewhere, and thus developed a counter motive. As we center our attention upon one thing or another, we largely determine our mental happiness and hence our bodily health. One person in walking through a noble forest, may search only for spiders and venomous creatures, while another confines his attention to the singing birds in the branches above."

From the above, it is seen that the only way to develop and maintain a free will is to direct the attention and thought by means of the awakened Ego—the Master Mind and Mind Master.

Positive and Negative Mentality

Most of us have heard the old proverb which states that "As a man thinketh, so is he." And most of us accept the spirit of the idea that a man's character, disposition, activities, and general personality are dependent largely upon the general character of his thoughts. This being so, and it also being true that a man is able to control the general character of his thoughts, it logically follows that every awakened Ego is the creator of the character and personality of the individual whose self it is.

Philosophers teach us that there is a law of polarity manifesting in everything. That is to say, that in everything there is found the presence of the two poles, viz., the positive and the negative. We find this law manifest in the mentality and character of every individual. There is always to be found the positive elements of mentality and character, and the negative elements thereof.

There is always to be the "two-sidedness" in individuals. Every individual finds within himself a constant struggle between these two opposing elements—the positive and the negative. Upon the decision of this battle depends largely the advancement, success, welfare, and progress of the individual. Goethe has well said: "In my breast, alas, two souls dwell, all there is unrest. Each with the other strives for mastery, each from the other struggles to be free." The ordinary individual seems to be content to remain as a passive spectator of this struggle; but the individual of the awakened Ego takes a part in the struggle, and by throwing the weight of his free will into the balance, he brings down the scales on the positive side.

But, you may ask, just what are the positive qualities? How may we know them when we consider them? This is a very natural, and a very proper question. As we proceed you will discover an infallible touchstone, or test whereby you may settle the matter for yourself. In most cases you will have no trouble in making the decision by the employment of your ordinary powers of judgment. For instance: you find no trouble in deciding that courage is positive, and cowardice negative; that truth is positive, and untruth negative; that energy is positive, and slothfulness is negative; that persistence is positive, and lack of it negative. But when you come to consider less familiar cases, you feel more or less uncertain, and instinctively look around for a touchstone or test, whereby you may decide infallibly.

A well-known writer, in considering this instinctive demand, has said: "When the individual is forced to consider any feeling, emotion, idea, action, advice, suggestion, or teaching, he should always submit it to the Touchstone of Positivity, by asking himself: 'Will this make me stronger, more powerful, more capable, more efficient, better?' In the degree that the thing corresponds to these qualifications, so is its degree of positivity. It becomes the duty of every individual wishing to progress on the Path of Life, and desiring to become proficient and capable in his expression and manifestation of mentality and character, to cultivate the positive qualities of the mind, and to restrain and inhibit the negative ones. In the consideration of this matter you should always remember that every positive quality has its negative opposite. This is an invariable rule, and one that you may test for yourself. And arising from it is this important rule of the new psychology: 'To develop a positive quality, you should restrain or inhibit its opposing negative: To restrain or inhibit a negative quality, you should develop and encourage its opposing positive.' The rule is worthy of being carved over the door of every institute of learning in the world, for its general observance would create a new race of men and women, and a new civilization of positive, capable, efficient people."

The positive qualities may be encouraged and developed by the mastery and control over the mental field exercised by the awakened Ego, and the negative qualities may be inhibited and restrained by the exercise of the same power within each individual. The Ego should always assert its positivity to the feelings, emotions, desires, and other mental states. The will should be held firmly in its place, as positive to the desires. The intellect should be held positive to the emotions, desires, and feelings. The Ego, through the will, should maintain a positive attitude toward, and control over, the attention and the imagination. True assertion of the Ego does not mean the petty quality called "egotism," but rather the higher phase of Egoism, or mastery of the Ego.

You are asked here to consider the following quotation from a well-known writer on the subject of the new psychology, who says: "Man should be more than a mere creature of chance, environment, and outside influences. He should be ruled from within—be self-ruled—by the power of the Ego. Instead of being merely a weak instrument of desire, emotion, and feeling, influenced by suggestions and impressions from every passing person or thing, man should be directed and guided by the strong instru-

Freud

ment of his will, held firmly to its task by the
Ego. With full power of regulation, decision,
and determination, and with the full will enforc-
ing those powers, man should be very giant of
endeavor and attainment, instead of the petty,
crawling, weakling that so many of his kind are
now. Man has it in his power to make of himself what he will—to become his own mental
creator, instead of allowing others to create his
mentality for him. Too long has man bowed
to environment and outer circumstances: he is
now learning to be his own environment, by
means of creating the same from within.

"The fundamental idea of the new psychology
is embodied in the symbol of the charioteer
driving his fiery steeds under full control and
with taut rein. The chariot represents the being
of the man; the charioteer, the Ego; the reins,
the will; the steeds, the mental states of feeling,
emotion, desire, imagination, and the rest. Unless the reins be strong, they will not be sufficient to control the horses. Unless the charioteer
be trained and vigilant, the horses will run away
with the chariot and dash to pieces the driver in
the general wreck. But controlled and mastered,
the fiery steeds will lead forward to attainment
and accomplishment, and at the same time will
travel the road in safety.

"Each of you is the charioteer driving the fiery steeds with the reins of the will. How are you driving? Are you mastering the steeds, or are they mastering you? It is in your power to curb, control, urge on, and direct these splendid mental creatures, so that you may travel far into the regions of attainment and accomplishment. Or, it is within your power to allow them to wander from side to side of the road, and into the swamps and morasses on the side. Or it is within your power to 'give them their heads' and to allow them to rush away with you to destruction. Have you decided which of the three courses you shall follow? Have you decided whether you shall be the Master, or the mastered? There comes a time in the life of each one of us when this question must be answered—the course chosen. It may be that this time has come to you in the reading of these lines. Are you ready to answer it, and to make the decision? Remember the question. It is this: 'Mastery or Servitude—Which?' "

Character Building depends upon the mental attitude and mental states of the individual. The man of positive thoughts and feelings will develop into the positive character; while he of negative thoughts and feelings will develop into the weakling, negative character. We usually lay great stress upon the axiom, "As a man thinketh, so is he," ignoring the correlated truth that as a man feeleth, so is he. But, at the last, when we see that a man's feelings are largely under his control and are really the outcome of his thoughts and the direction of his attention, the truth of the first axiom becomes doubly apparent.

Character building depends greatly upon the "feeling" side of his mental nature. Pure abstract thinking may serve to prevent negative feelings, but other than this it has little or no positive value in character building. But when the man is thinking about anything in which his interest, his feelings, his emotions, his desire, or his passions are involved, then we find that he is building character for good or evil. Hence the importance of the man's interests being directed toward positive things, rather than to the negative ones.

The formation of positive ideals has much to do with the building up of a positive character. A man grows to resemble his ideas. And a man's ideals are the outgrowth of his feelings and emotions. The ideal hold by the man arouses interest in all things connected with it. Interest is the strong motive of attention; and attention is the beginning of all the activities of the will. So the man's ideals serve to set into activity the chain of mental cause and effect that results in storing away in his mind the strong impressions that have so much to do with the building up of character. By the constant use of these impressions, he builds up the mental path of habit over which the will so likes to travel. And the more frequently he uses these mental paths, the more does his character become "set." So we find over fresh illustrations of the statement that "A man tends to grow to resemble the things he likes, and in which he is interested." So true is this that a writer has suggested that we say "As a man loveth, so is he." But here again the Master Mind assorts its power, and says: "I love that which I want to love—I am free here as in all else in my realm." But, though this last be so, the man's likes and his ideals are important pieces of the machinery by means of which he builds up his character.

Modern psychology teaches us that the two following principles are operative in the character of each individual, viz.: (1) That feelings manifest themselves in will action unless inhibited or controlled; and (2) that the will-action follows the lines of the strongest interest. These twin principles of mental action should be considered together.

The first of the above named principles, i.e., the principle that feelings manifest themselves in action unless inhibited or controlled, is recognized as a fact by all leading psychologists of today. William James has said concerning it: "All consciousness is motor. We might say that every possible feeling produces a movement, and that the movement is a movement of the entire organism, and of each and all of its parts. If we fancy some strong emotion, and then try to abstract from our consciousness of it all the feelings of its bodily symptoms, we find that we have nothing left behind." There is always the tendency toward outward expression and manifestation of all feelings, emotions, desires, and passions, which tendency proceeds into action unless controlled or inhibited. This being perceived, it is seen that our actions (and consequently our character) tend to fall into the pattern or mold created by those of our feelings and desires which are permitted to survive and remain uncontrolled.

We constantly act, often unconsciously, in accordance with our strongest desires, feelings, likes or dislikes, prejudices, etc., all of which are but phases of feeling. Our physical lives are regulated by our mental states, and our mental states are largely what we make them—providing that we have learned the art and science of

Mental Mastery. The materials of our feelings are taken from the subconscious mental storehouse, and what comes out of that plane of our mentality must have previously gone into it. The Master Mind recognizes this and places in that storehouse only what he chooses to go into it, and what he chooses to come out of it as the incentive to action—being always governed in his choice by the Rule of Positivity heretofore announced, viz.: "Will this make me stronger, more powerful, more capable, more efficient, better?" By stocking the subconscious storehouse with positive material, only positive material will be issued therefrom to form the basis of actions.

The second of the above named principles, i.e., the principle that the will-action follows the lines of the strongest interest, is likewise recognized as correct by the best authorities. The majority of persons follow the line of the least resistance, and allow their interest to become attracted and held by many things which have no positive value to the individual, and which too often has a decidedly negative character. The few who have experienced the consciousness of the awakened Ego, and who have at least begun to assert the Master Mind, act intelligently in this matter and refuse to place the interest upon any negative thing, or anything lacking a positive value to them.

An authority has said: "To many persons the suggestion that they have the power to select the objects of their interest may seem absurd. They are so accustomed to regard interest, feelings, desires, and emotions, and even passions, as things beyond their control, that they make no attempt to exercise a voluntary control over them. It is true that these mental states do not spring from pure intellectual effort—that they spring from the depths of the subconscious mentality, unbidden, in most cases. But the proved facts of the new psychology show us plainly that the Ego may assume control of these involuntary metal states, and either encourage and develop them, or else restrain or inhibit them entirely. Just as the will may assume control of certain muscles of the body, so may the Ego assume control of the entire mental kingdom, and mold, build, change, and improve each and every department of its mental workshop. By concentration and attention, interest may be directed to and held upon certain things, and likewise removed or kept away from certain things. Interest kindles desire, and lack of interest causes desire to die. And interest results from attention, and may be controlled by the will And the will is the chief instrument of the Ego. By using the reasoning and judicial faculties of the mind in the matter of the right selection of objects of interest, the positive qualities and objects may be selected in preference to the negative ones. And this being done, we are well started on our way toward character building, mastery and power."

In the following pages of this book the reader will be asked to consider each particular set of mental faculties, and each particular phase of mental activity and expression. The special machinery of each set or phase thereof will be analyzed, and the part played by it in the mental life of the individual will be described and explained. At the same time the reader will be instructed in the most approved methods whereby each of these set of faculties, or phases of mentality, may be brought and held under the control of the Ego, by the use of the will, and those be brought into the category of Positive Mentality.

Common belief to the contrary notwithstanding, every individual is the possible architect and builder of his own mental character—though but few really exercise that power. Too often we are told that a man's character is entirely molded by Circumstances. We lose sight of the spirit of that great Master of Mind who exclaimed: "Circumstances! I make Circumstances!" The

Positive Mentality always is stronger than the Negative Mentality, and is able to direct, control, and master the latter. Hence the power of the Master Minds of the race over the Slave Minds of the herd of the masses of the race.

Before proceeding to the detailed consideration of the several mental faculties, and phases of mental activity, let us consider the following quotation from a popular writer on the subject of mind power. This writer once said to his students, concluding a series of lessons to them:

"If you are an individual, this teaching is just what you want. And the same is true if you are not one, but want to be one. But if you are a weakling, and prefer to remain one, instead of rising and claiming your birthright of strength—your heritage of power, then by all means remain as you are, and go on your own way. Leave these teachings for the others of your brethren, who will not sell their birthright of power for the mess of pottage of negative content and sheep-like passivity, but who are boldly claiming their own, and demanding their rightful portion—these strong brothers of yours, the individuals who are the coming inheritors of the earth. I send to you, who are now reading these words, all the energy, force, and power at my command, to the end that it may pierce your armor of indifference, fear, and doubt. And that, reaching into your heart of desire it may fill you with the very spirit of individuality, conscious ego-hood, perception of reality, and realization of the Ego. So that henceforth your battle-cry will be changed, and you will plunge into the thick of the fight, filled with the Berserker rage of attainment like the Icelandic hero of old, shouting your positive battle-cry of freedom, 'I can, I will; I dare, I do! you will mow your way clear through the ranks of the horde of ignorance, find negativity, and reach the heights beyond. This is my message to YOU, the Individual!"

We trust that the reader of this book will "catch the spirit" of the above message, and will carry it with him through his study of the following pages of this book—for this, indeed, truly expresses the spirit of the Positive Mentality of the Master Mind.

The Senses and Sensations

It is usual to begin all teaching concerning the mind by a general discourse upon "the senses." This is, indeed, the only logical approach to the main subject, for the impressions received by us through the senses—the '' sensations"—have well been called "the raw materials of mental activities." It is well that the Master Mind become acquainted with these "raw materials" which it expects to use.

In popular usage the term "sense" is commonly employed as identical with '' understanding," or "reason"; but in psychology the term has a far more restricted meaning. In psychology the term "sense" has the following meaning: "The faculty possessed by conscious creatures whereby they perceive external objects by means of impressions made upon certain organs of the body, or whereby they receive impressions concerning changes in the condition of the body." The term "sensation," in psychology, is defined as: "An impression made upon the mind through the medium of the nervous system, and usually through one of the organs of sense."

The senses are usually regarded as consisting of five general classes, each with its appropriate organism of sensation, as follows:

The Sense of Touch, or Feeling

The sense of Touch, or Feeling, is regarded by psychologists as the elementary sense—the one sense from which the others have evolved, and of which they are, in a way, an evolution. The sense of Touch, or Feeling, operates by means of certain nerves which have their endings in the outer covering or skin of the body, and also in the internal organism of the body. These nerves report to the mind their contact with outside objects; and, in some cases, certain changes of state or condition in the body itself. By means of this sense we are able to become aware of the size, form, shape and delight of material objects; of their degree of hardness, roughness, elasticity, etc.; of their temperature; and of other physical characteristics by which we distinguish one material object from another by means of respective reaction to our sense of Touch or Feeling. By means of this sense we also become aware of changes of state or condition in our bodies, such as thirst, hunger, sexual-feeling, and other "internal sensations."

The mechanism of the sense of Touch, or Feeling, is composed of many different and varied classes of nerve channels. This being so, the sense of Touch, or Feeling, is really a composite sense, manifesting diverse activities, principal among which are those of pressure, temperature, muscular resistance, pain, contact, etc. This diversity of activity is illustrated of the physiology of the senses: "A lesion which may cut off the possibility of feeling pain in a given part of the body, may leave it still susceptible to sensations of heat and cold; or the sensations of touch may be present while the sensation of pain cannot be aroused. From this we see that nerve impulses, giving rise to sensations of touch, of pain, of temperature, of the muscular sense, must pass upwards to the sensorium by different paths, one of which may be cut off while the others remain."

The Sense of Sight
The sense of Sight, regarded by psychologists as an evolution of the elementary sense of Touch or Feeling, is regarded by the best authorities as the highest in the scale of the evolved senses. It manifests through a most complex organism and nerve- arrangement. The sense of Sight operates by means of registering the sensations of the intensity of the light waves, and the color vibrations thereof. The eye does not touch or feel the outside objects in order to "see" them; instead, it "touches" or "feels" the vibrations of the lightwaves coming in contact with the nervous matter of the organ of sight.

A leading text book on the subject of physiology describes the mechanism of the organ of sight as follows: "The optical apparatus may be supposed for the sake of description to consist of several parts. First, of a system of transparent refracting surfaces and media by means of which images of external objects are brought to a focus upon the back of the eye; and, secondly, of a sensitive screen, the retina, which is a specialized termination of the optic nerve, capable of being stimulated by luminous objects, and of sending through the optic nerve such an impression as to produce in the brain visual sensations. To these main parts may be added, thirdly, an apparatus for focusing objects at different distances from the eye, called 'accommodation.' Even this does not complete the description of the whole organ of vision, since both eyes are usually employed in vision; and forthly, an arrangement exists by means of which the eyes may be turned in the same direction by a system of muscles, so that binocular vision is possible. The eye may be compared to a photographic camera, and the transparent media corresponds to the photographic lens. In such a camera images of objects are thrown upon a ground-glass screen at the back of a box, the interior of which is painted black. In the eye, the camera proper is represented by the eyeball with its choroidal pigment, the screen by the retina, and the lens by the refracting media. In the ease of the camera, the screen is enabled to receive clear images of objects at different distances, by an apparatus for focusing. The corresponding contrivance in the eye is the 'accommodation.' The iris, which is capable of allowing more or less light to pass into the eye, corresponds with the different-sized diaphragms used in photographic apparatus." The "retina" of the eye, above mentioned, is a very sensitive membrane of nerve-matter lining the back of the eye, and being connected with the minute ends of the optic nerve; from the retina the impression is conveyed by the nerves to the brain.

The Sense of Taste

The sense of Taste, another evolved sense, manifests by means of certain nerves terminating in tiny cells of the tongue, known as "taste buds"; the latter are stimulated chemically by objects brought in contact with them, the impulse being conveyed to the nerves, and by them transmitted to the brain. Physiologists classify the sensations of taste into five classes, viz., sweet, sour, bitter, salty, and "hot" (as in the case of pepper, etc.).

The Sense of Smell

The sense of Smell, another evolved sense, manifests by means of delicate nerves terminating in the mucus membrane of the nostrils; the latter registering contact with minute particles of material objects entering the nostrils, and also registering differences in the chemical composition of such particles; the message of the nerve ends being transmitted to the brain. The particles of the "smelled" object must have actually entered the nostrils and have come in contact with these nerve ends in order to have been sensed. Mere nearness to the organ of smell is not sufficient—actual contact must be had, or we will smell nothing. We "smell" the rose only because minute particles of its substance are carried into our nostrils. We smell gas because some of its particles enter our nostrils.

The Sense of Hearing

The sense of Hearing, another evolved sense, manifest by means of delicate nerve terminating in the inner part of the ear. The eardrum, or "tympanum," vibrates in response to the air-vibrations or sound-waves reaching it from the outside; these vibrations are intensified, and the auditory nerve-ends take up the impression and pass it on to the brain. Sound-waves are sensed according to their characteristics of pitch, intensity, quality, and harmony, respectively.

The Offices of the Senses

The senses constitute the doors to the outside world, which when opened permit the entrance of messages from that world, but which, closed, bar the entrance of anything from without. Few of us ever stop to think how completely we are dependent upon these doors of the senses for our knowledge, our experience, and our objects of thought. We take it all for granted, and fail to perceive the importance of these senses. Only when one or more of the senses fail us do we begin to realize their importance, and the importance of sensations as a whole. It is only when we stop to think how completely shut in, and shut out, we would be if all of our senses were destroyed, that we begin to realize just how dependent we are upon the senses and sensation for our knowledge, our thoughts, our feelings, and our general mental life and being.

A leading psychologist has said: "Suppose a child of intelligent parents were ushered into the world without a nerve leading from his otherwise perfect brain to any portion of his body; with no optic nerve to transmit the glorious sensations from the eye, no auditory nerve to conduct the vibrations of the mother's voice, no tactile nerves to convey the touch of a hand, no olfactory nerve to rouse the brain with the delicate aroma of the orchards and the wild flowers in spring, no gustatory, thermal, or muscular nerves. Could such a child live, as the years rolled on, the books of Shakespeare and of Milton would be opened in vain before the child's eyes. The wisest men might talk to him with utmost eloquence all to no purpose. Nature could not whisper one of her inspiring truths into his deaf ear, could not light up that dark mind with a picture of the rainbow or of a human face. No matter how perfect might be the child's brain and his inherited capacity for mental activities, his faculties would remain for this life shrouded in Egyptian darkness. Perception could give memory nothing to retain, and thought could not weave her matchless fabrics without materials."

Another psychologist has said: "If it were possible for a human being to come into the world with a brain perfectly prepared to be the instrument of psychical operations, but with all the inlets to sensations closed, we have every reason to believe that the mind would remain dormant like a seed buried in the earth." Another says: "That the powers of the understanding would forever continue dormant were it not for the action of things external to the body, is a proposition now universally admitted by philosophers." Another says: "Apprehension by the senses supplies directly or indirectly the material of all human knowledge, or at least the stimulus necessary to develop every inborn faculty of the mind." Another says: "Even the highest ideas are slowly and gradually developed from the accumulation of sense experiences, and their truth is only guaranteed by the possibility of finding concrete examples for them in real existence. Another says: "The activity of the mind is just as much the result of its consciousness of external impressions, by which its faculties are called into play, as the life of the body is dependent upon the appropriation of nutrient materials and the constant influence of external forces." And another: "The senses are the means by which the mind obtains its knowledge of the outside world. Shut out from all direct communication with the outer world, it knows, and can know, nothing of what exists or is passing there, except what comes to it through the senses. Its knowledge of what is external to itself is therefore dependent upon the number, state, and condition of the sensory organs."

In short: Psychologists hold that if a human being were born without sense organs, no matter how perfect a brain he might have, his life would be little more than that of the plant. He would exist in a dreamlike state, with only the faintest manifestations of consciousness. His consciousness would not be able to react in response to the impact of contact with the outside world, for there would be no such impact. And as consciousness depends almost entirely upon the impact of, or resistance to, outside impressions, his power of consciousness would be practically not called into play. He would perhaps be conscious of his own existence, but would probably never realize the fact fully, for he would have nothing else with which to compare himself, and his self-consciousness would not be aroused by the presence and pressure of the "not self." Such a man would not even have the memories of previous sensations, or experiences, to arouse or to heighten his consciousness or thought—and, consequently, he would have no imagination to use. He would be, to all intents and purposes, a "living corpse."

Helen Keller had only two doors of sensation closed to her—the sense of Sight and that of Hearing. Touch, Taste, and Smell, however, were left to her; and each was quickened and heightened in order to help as far as possible to perform the work properly belonging to the defective senses. Her sense of Touch, especially, was wonderfully increased and quickened into activity; and through this channel her "self" was finally reached and communicated with by loving friends and teachers. The result in this particular case was almost a miracle—yet only two senses were missing. To get the full realization of the importance of the senses, one had but to think of the mental state of a Helen Keller deprived from birth of the sense of Touch!

Arising from the above line of thought is the realization, that just as the world of the individual is decreased by each sense subtracted from him, so would his world be increased by each sense that might be added to him. And daring minds consider it not improbable that the human race, in the course of evolution, may eventually develop other and more complex senses. Even as it is, man is able to perceive only a limited number of sound sensations—there are many sounds above and below his scale that he is unable to perceive, but which are registered on instruments. Likewise, there are light waves below and above the human scale of perception, but which are caught by delicate instruments. And, at present, man is unable to "sense" electrical waves, or magnetic waves—though, theoretically, it is possible for him to sense these vibrations as well as light waves, or sound waves, the difference between these various "waves" being simply that of the rate of vibration. Imagine what a new world would be opened to man if he could sense the waves of electricity. In that case he could "see" things as far off as these waves could carry, and even though solid objects intervened—just as now, by means of an artificial screen, he is able to see through solid objects by means of the X-Ray. This is by no means a fanciful idea.

A leading authority has said: "If a new sense or two were added to the present normal number, in man, that which is now the phenomenal world for all of us might, for all that we know, burst into something amazingly different and wider, in consequence of the additional revelation of these new senses." And another says: "It is not at all improbable that there are properties of matter of which none of our senses take immediate cognizance, and which other beings might be able to see in the same manner that we are sensible to light, sound, etc." Another says: ""We know that our sensory nerves are capable of transmitting to the brain only a part of the phenomena of the universe. Our senses give us only a section of the world's phenomena. Our senses usher only certain phenomena into the presence of our minds. If we had three or four new senses added, this might appear like a new world to us; we might become conscious of a vast number of phenomena, which at present never have any effect upon our nervous organisms. It is possible to imagine a race of beings whose senses do not resemble ours, inhabiting other worlds."

A fanciful illustration of the part played by the senses in our mental world is offered by a writer who says: "The late Professor James once suggested as a useful exercise for young students a consideration of the changes which would be worked in our ordinary world if the various branches of our receiving instruments happened to exchange duties; if, for instance, we heard all colors, and saw all sounds. All this is less mad than it seems. Music is but an interpretation of certain vibrations undertaken by the ear, and color but an interpretation of other vibrations undertaken by the eye. Were such an alteration of our senses to take place, the world would still be sending us the same messages, but we should be interpreting them differently. Beauty would still be ours, though speaking another tongue. The birds' song would then strike our retina as a pageant of color: we should see all the magical tones of the wind, hear as a great fugue the repeated and harmonized greens of the forest, the cadences of stormy skies. Did we realize how slight an adjustment of our own organs is needed to initiate us into such a world, we should perhaps be less contemptuous of those mystics who tell us that in moments of transcendental conscious they 'heard flowers that sounded, and saw notes that shone,' or that they have experienced rare moments of consciousness in which the senses were fused into a single and ineffable act of perception, in which color and sound were known as aspects of the same thing."

As has been said, at the last all of the five senses are regarded by physiologists and psychologists as but different aspects or phases of the one elemental and basic sense, the Sense of Feeling. This is more fully realized when we consider that all impressions made upon the organs of sense arise from the motion of material particles, from the outside world, coming in contact with sensitive portions of the nervous system of the individual, the report of the contact being then transmitted to his brain. As an authority has said: "The only way the external world affects the nervous system is by means motion. Light is motion; sound is motion; heat is motion; touch is motion; taste and smell are motion. The world is known to sense simply by virtue of, and in relation to, the motion of its particles. Those motions are appreciated and continued by the nervous system, and by it brought at length to the mind's perception. The last material action we can trace in every process of sensation previous to its entering the abode of consciousness is motion."

And so, at the last, we are conscious of these different forms of motion of things of the outside world by some form of the sense of Feeling. Sight is but the feeling of the impact of the light vibrations; Sound, but the feeling of the impact of the sound vibrations; Taste, but the feeling of the vibrations of chemical action of the particles of material substances brought in contact with the taste-nerves; Smell, but the impact of the particles of material substance brought in contact with the nerves of smell; Touch, but the feeling of the contact with outside physical objects; and Internal Feelings but the feeling of certain states of conditions of the internal organs or parts of the body of the individual. And so, we see that the various sensations are all but forms or phases of the "feeling" arising from the contact with certain sensitive nerve- ends with outside things, and the transmission of such report to the brain.

When these reports to the brain are made, the sense impression becomes a full "sensation." An authority says: "A sensation is a state of consciousness resulting from nerve action. When a stimulation of a sensory nerve is transmitted to the brain, so as to affect consciousness, the result is a sensation. No one can tell us why nerve action affects consciousness, but such is the fact." And here we come into the presence of the great mystery of consciousness. Consciousness is different from anything else in the world of our knowledge or experience. It can be known only to itself and by itself, but even itself does not know "just what" it is, or how it is. As Huxley, the eminent scientist once said: "How it is that anything so remarkable as a state of consciousness comes about by the result of irritating nervous tissue, is just as unaccountable as the presence of the genie when Aladdin rubbed his lamp." We shall in this book make no attempt to tell "just what" consciousness is, but shall content ourselves with telling our readers "just how" it works, and how to use it efficiently and to the best advantage.

We have here seen the mechanism of the senses whereby the Ego is established in communication with the outside world. Dwelling alone in calm solitude, the Ego is constantly receiving the messages from without its dwelling place, as well as from the different rooms of its own place of abode. Telegraph and telephone lines run into that central office, from all directions—telescopes and other optical appliances are trained to all points—heat-registering, light-registering, sound-registering, and motion- registering instruments are at hand and in constant use. All these instruments have been furnished by Nature for the use of the Ego—or, as some prefer to state it, the Ego has fashioned these instruments to meet its requirements.

And, always remember this: It is the Ego who feels, the Ego who smells, the Ego who tastes, the Ego who hears, the Ego who sees—and not the sense organs which have been described in this chapter. And if other channels of sensation are opened up to the Ego, or by the Ego, in the future evolution of the race, it will then be the Ego who perceives through them. Back of all sensations is the Ego—the Subject to which all the rest is objective.

The Culture of the Senses

The senses may be cultivated in two general ways, as follows: (1) By maintaining the sense organs in a state of perfect health and normal functioning; (2) by employing each sense by means of the voluntary attention, according to the universal "Law of Use" which operates so as to develop and perfect the physical organs and parts, and the mental faculties, in response to the demands made upon them by Use and Active Employment. The first of the above mentioned methods are outside of the field and scope of this book, and the student is referred to works along the general lines of physiology and physical well-being for detailed information on this score. The second of the above mentioned methods will be considered in detail as we proceed in this book to a consideration of the subjects of Perception and Attention, respectively.

Here is the thing in a nutshell: The senses may be cultivated and rendered more efficient by (a) giving the sense-organism the proper physical care and attention, and by (b) employing the senses intelligently and toward definite ends under the direction of the will. And the latter is a task of the Master Mind.

Perception

In the preceding chapter your attention was directed toward the subject of the Senses and Sensations. You will remember that in that chapter Sensations were spoken of as the "raw materials of mental activities." In the present chapter your attention is directed toward the inner phase of Sensation—the conscious recognition of Sensations—which is known in psychology as Perception. The Master Mind has in Perception a valuable servant—if it be well trained.

Here, please note the distinction between the two: Sensation is the impression conveyed to the mind, from the outside of the limits of the mind, through the medium of the nervous system, and usually through one of the organs of the senses; Perception is the act of consciousness, performed within the limits of the mind, whereby it becomes conscious of the impression of Sensation, and starts to "know" the latter. You may be helped in grasping the distinction by making a mental note of the following statement, viz.: Sensation is a feeling; Perception is the thought resulting from that feeling. Perception interprets the report of Sensation, and translates it into a Thought, or Idea.

Sensation is simple, and depends upon the sensory mechanism; while Perception is a higher and more complex mental process, depending for its efficiency not only upon the degree and attention given to the impression or Sensation, but also upon previous experience and training. It would be noted that one may receive an impression through one or more of the senses, and yet fail to interpret or translate that impression into a conscious Perception, or act of knowing.

We do not perceive all the impressions of the senses; we do not know all our sensations. Out of a multitude of sounds reaching our sense of hearing, we may take notice of only one and interpret it by Perception. Our sense of sight may receive the impressions of many sight-sensations, and yet take notice of and interpret only one of the number. "Walking down a busy street, our eyes register thousands of impressions, but how few of them awaken attention in our minds and result in our perceiving the impression? Unless our attention is attracted toward the impression, we fail to perceive it. Many persons go through life seeing and hearing much, but perceiving very little. Likewise, habit and familiarity may dull the perception. The novelty of a new impression may attract our attention, and arouse perception at first. But "seen too oft," the object causing the impression fails to attract our attention; we begin to fail to notice the impression, and finally may even fail to perceive it at all.

It may as well be stated at this point that in Attention—that wonderful power of the mind, and the one which is the chief tool of the Master Mind—lies the secret of efficient Perception. You will have your attention positively directed toward the subject of Attention as we proceed, and until that point is reached you are asked to note how often the term is employed in connection with Perception. Attention is the key to the mastery of Perception. Withdraw Attention, and Perception practically is paralyzed. We shall see the reason for this presently; in the meantime we ask that you take it for granted.

But more than Attention is required in the act of Perception. The previous experience and mental training of the person manifest results in the process of full Perception. For instance: A gun is fired at a distance. One man, being busy with other things, fails to have his Attention awakened, and so remains in practical ignorance of the happening. The second man has his attention awakened, and registers a simple perception of the impressions; but, having had no previous experience with guns or explosions, he does not fully interpret into Perception the sensation; he perceives "noise," but not "the report of a gun." The third man, having had experience with the report of a gun, interprets the sensation into the Perception of the sensation as "the report of a gun." The fourth man, being well acquainted with the incidents of gun-firing, and being somewhat of an expert on the subject, interprets the sensation so fully that he perceives and knows it to he not only "the report of a gun," but also whether it be the report of a rifle or shot gun, as the case may be, and also, possibly, the size and caliber of the gun. And yet, note you this, the sensation of sound was precisely the same in each and every case, notwithstanding that perception and the knowing varied materially in the several hearers of that sound-sensation.

All the mental powers of the individual are represented in the act of Perception. The memory plays an important part in determining the report of the impression, for all experience and training is registered in the memory, and is called from it when one strives to manifest Perception. Moreover, the discrimination and judgment are called into activity in order to determine "just what" the impression of the sensation may be. The mental processes of the infant give us an excellent example of the growth and development of Perception. At first, "all things look alike to me" to the infant; but the child soon learns to perceive differences between things, and to manifest his knowledge of such differences. Sensation is more or less mechanical; but Perception results from experience, training, and thought processes.

The human child is not born with the perception of Space. At first all things seem to the infant to be equally near or equally far; he stretches out his hands to grasp some distant object, the moon for instance, and cries because he cannot reach it. But in time, gradually, and by experience and experiment, he acquires the perception of the distance and space between things. A person born blind, and afterward having his sight awakened by means of an operation, experiences the same difficulty—he must educate his perception to interpret his sensations of sight. One may have a very keen sense, but unless his perception be developed he will not be able to have an intelligent conception of the things impressed upon him through the sense of sight. A blind man knows a cat by means of his perception of touch-sensation, but when his sight is restored he does not recognize the cat as a cat when he sees it, but must first identify it by touching it and then correlating the impressions of sight and touch before he can recognize and interpret the sight-sensations.

Perhaps some of our readers will be able to get this distinction established more clearly by reference to the familiar example of a crowd of men and women gazing at a woman who is passing them. The men and the women will receive precisely the same sense impression or sensation of the passing woman; but ask them afterward and you will realize the difference in their respective perceptions arising from the same series of sense-impressions, or sensations. You will find that the men will have perceived merely the general appearance of the woman, some perhaps having perceived whether or not she was pretty, dressed stylishly, etc.—in short, the points regarding the woman which have specially interested them. The women of the crowd, however, will be found to have perceived many details regarding the woman's apparel and general appearance; they will have perceived the precise degree of "make up" on the woman's face, the quality and general value of the material in her gown, the details of the trimming thereof, etc., as well as the quality and degree of stylishness of her hat, its trimming, and its probable price. And yet all—men and women alike— will have received precisely the same sense-impressions or sensations arising from the presence of the passing woman.

The reason for the different degrees of perception noted in the example just given is largely that covered by the definition of the term "Apperception," one quite in favor with modern psychologists. Apperception consists, in the main, of the association of the present Perception with others previously experienced; in short, the present perception takes a degree of color from those previously experienced, and, moreover, the color of the previous Perceptions tend to shut out or neutralize other colors inherent in the present Perception. (The word "color" is used here merely in the figurative sense, of course.)

A leading psychologist has well illustrated the action and effect of Apperception in the following story: "A boy concealed himself in a tree and watched the passers. When one man remarked to a friend what a fine stick of timber the tree would make, the boy said: 'Good morning, Mr. Carpenter.' Soon another passed said: 'That is good bark.' 'Good morning, Mr. Tanner.' Presently a young man remarked: 'I'll venture there's a squirrel's nest in that tree.' 'Good morning, Mr. Hunter.' In one sense those men saw exactly the same tree, had the same sensations of color and light from the same object; but from the way the men apperceived the tree, the boy was able to tell their leading vocations. Each apperceived the tree in terms of his most prominent experience. In one sense Perception is an apperceiving process, for each new sensation is biased by previous sensations; each new perception, by previous perceptions. Association is one form of apperception; thinking, another."

There is a great difference between the power of Perception of different individuals, the difference depending very little, comparatively, on the difference in the keenness of the sense organs of the persons, but depending very largely upon the degree of attention which the different persons place upon their sense-impressions, and upon the degree of training they have given their perceptive faculties. That this has a vital relation to the degree of intelligent thought and general knowledge of the different individuals may be gathered from the following quotation from a well-known psychologist, who says: "Perception is the immediate source of our knowledge of outside objects, and in that sense is the cause thereof. Perception also furnishes the understanding with materials out of which it derives ideas and truths beyond the field of sense. As thus attaining a knowledge of external objects, affording material for the operation of the understanding, and furnishing the occasion for the activity of the intuitive power, Perception may be said to lie at the basis of all knowledge."

The great majority of persons are very careless observers. They will see things without perceiving the qualities, properties, characteristics, or parts which together make up these things. Two persons, possessed of equal degrees of eye-sight, will perceive quite different qualities in the same thing, or differing degrees of the same quality. One person perceives merely "a pile of stone," while another will perceive a pile of granite or marble, and may possibly perceive the quality and quantity thereof. Another will perceive merely "a tree," while another will distinguish the kind of tree it is, and also many particulars concerning the bark, leaves, trunk, etc., thereof.

A psychologist says of this: "Very few persons can tell the difference between the number of legs of a fly and a spider; and I have known farmers' boys and girls who could not tell whether the ears of a cow are in front of her horns, above her horns, below her horns, or behind her horns." Another psychologist says: "Fifteen pupils in a school-room were sure that they had seen cats climb trees and descend them. There was a unanimity of opinion that the cats went up head first. When asked whether the cats came down head or tail first, the majority were sure that the cats descended as they were never known to do. Anyone who had ever noticed the shape of the claws of any beast of prey could have answered that question without seeing an actual descent. Farmers' boys who have often seen cows and horses lie down and rise, are seldom sure whether the animals rise with their fore or hind feet first, or whether the habit of the horse agrees with that of the cow in this respect."

As a leading psychologist has well said: "Modern education has tended to the neglect of the culture of the perceptive powers. In ancient times people studied nature much more than at present. Being without books they were compelled to depend upon their eyes and ears for knowledge; and this made their senses active, searching and exact. At the present day, we study books for a knowledge of external things; and we study them too much or too exclusively, and thus neglect the cultivation of the senses. We get our knowledge of the material world second-hand, instead of fresh from the open pages of the book of nature. Is it not a great mistake to spend so much time in school and yet not be able to tell the difference between the leaf of a beech and of an oak; or not to be able to distinguish between specimens of marble, quartz, and granite? The neglect of culture of the perceptive powers is shown by the scholars of the present time. Very few educated men are good observers; indeed, most of them are sadly deficient in this respect. They were taught to think and remember, but were not taught to use their eyes and ears. In modern education, books have been used too much like spectacles, and the result is the blunting of the natural powers of perception."

The Master Mind is a Master Perceiver, for unless it were so it would not be a Master in the rest of the mental field. A psychologist has well pictured the Master Mind, as follows: "It is a self-conscious activity and not a mere passivity. It is a center of spiritual forces, all resting in the background of the Ego. As a center of forces, it stands related to the forces of the material and spiritual universe, and is acted upon through its susceptibilities by those forces. As a spiritual activity, it takes impressions derived from those forces, works them up into the organic growth of itself, converts them into conscious knowledge, and uses these products as means to set other forces into activity and produce new results. Standing above nature, and superior to its surroundings, it nevertheless feeds upon nature, as we may say, and transforms material influences into spiritual facts akin to its own nature. Related to the natural world, and apparently originating from it, it yet rises above this natural world and, with the crown of freedom upon its brow, rules the natural world obedient to its will."

As we proceed we shall give the reader of this book full and detailed information concerning the Culture and Development of Perception. But, before entering upon that phase of the subject, we wish the reader to become acquainted with the possibilities of such culture and development. Perhaps the best way to illustrate and make clear these possibilities, is to point to specific and particular examples thereof— and the world about us is filled with such examples, as we will find if we will but look for them. An ordinary example is related by a psychologist who says: "It is related to a teacher that if, when hearing a class, some one rapped at the door, he would look up as the visitor entered and from a single glance could tell his appearance and dress, the kind of hat he wore, kind of necktie, collar, vest, coat, shoes, etc. The skillful banker, also, in counting money with wondrous rapidity, will detect and throw away from his pile of bills the counterfeits which, to the ordinary eye, seem to be without spot or blemish."

We shall now present to your attention a number of instances of interesting and somewhat

unusual cultivation and employment of the
faculty of Perception, which are taken from the
work upon "Memory Training" from the pen
of the writer of the present book, and in which
book the said examples are employed to point
out the possibilities of Memory Culture through
cultivation of Perception, for the two phases
of mental activity have a close connection
one with the other. Here follow the quotations
above mentioned:

Sight-Perception
Herschel states that the mosaic workers at the
Vatican were able to distinguish correctly between thirty thousand different shades, tints,
and hues of color. Ordinary artists distinguish
fine shades, tints, and hues of colors that are
imperceptible to the ordinary person; the difference being solely a difference of degree of
interest, attention, and practice. A person familiar with engraving will detect the most minute
points of difference in prints, engravings, etc.
Persons familiar with engraved banknotes are
able to detect counterfeits at a glance, even in
cases where the ordinary eye fails to detect the
slightest difference from the original. Experts in
handwriting are able not only to recognize the
handwriting of the individual, and to distinguish
the same from forgeries thereof, but are also
able to detect the characteristics of the hand-

writing even when the writers strive to disguise this; and they are able even to recognize the mental and physical condition of the individual at the time of the writing, solely from an examination of specimens of writing from his pen at such time. These points of difference are of course not perceived by the ordinary person.

Houdini, the great French conjurer, deliberately developed his memory and powers of visual perception, by certain methods, that he was able to pass rapidly by a shop window, taking but one sharp glance at its contents, and then, out of sight of the window, he could give a list, practically complete, of the various articles, displayed in the window, even to the most trifling objects. More than this, he taught his assistant to do the same thing. This would seem almost incredible were it not verified by the best authority.

It is related of several well-known artists, that they had developed their visual perception to such a high degree that they would grasp all the little points of a person's appearance at one glance, and afterward be able to reproduce with paint on canvass. Several celebrated bets based on this power are recorded in the history of the lives of eminent artists. A familiar instance of this class of perception is found among many women of fashion, as everyone knows. They are able to give a quick glance at the wearing apparel of other women, and thus take in the perception of the costume to the most minute detail, afterward reciting the same perfectly. I have known many women, personally, who had developed this faculty to an almost incredible degree of perfection.

Akin to this is the visual perception of certain well-paid observers of the milliners and customers of the large cities. Gaining access to the rooms of rivals in trade, they will sweep the contents of the showcases in a single glance, and in that glance will perceive not only the general style, but also the details of trimming, ornamentation, decoration, etc., so perfectly that they will be able to reproduce the same at their leisure in the workshops of their employers. Large shops in the leading cities of the civilized world employ trained observers of this class, who promenade through the aisles of the shops of their competitors, taking full and detailed mental notes of new styles, improvements, etc., their identity of course being carefully concealed as a matter of policy. This form of trained observation is particularly in favor in the large American cities; in fact, the American observers of this kind are said to excel all others in this faculty of photographic visual perception, and the reproduction thereof, and they frequently receive very high salaries for this skilled work. It is said of some of the best of these observers, that if they be given the opportunity and time for merely a single comprehensive glance at a new gown, they will be able to describe in detail the interesting and distinctive points of the gown, and to direct the reconstruction of a duplicate thereof in the workshops of their own establishment.

It is a well known fact that professional thieves in the large cities of the world employ apprentices as observers. These observers are disguised as beggars, messengers, errand boys, etc., who visit places designed to be the scenes of future robberies. They take a hasty glance at the premises, carefully noting the location of the several doors, windows, locks, etc., which they afterward note on paper. From these notes a map is constructed, which gives the thieves a great advantage in the matter of efficient entry, quick work, and safe escape, when the crime is actually committed.

Spies and detectives in the employ of the secret service of the various nations usually have this faculty well developed—sometimes to a wonderful degree. I personally have been informed by a high official of a certain government that he has in his employ a female spy who is able to perceive an entire page of a letter at a single glance, and to afterward reproduce its contents from memory. This would seem incredible were it not supported by records of many other cases of a similar nature. In fact, such a faculty may be developed by any person of ordinary perception, if he will but devote enough time, work, and interest to the task. Many readers of books really visualize entire lines of the book, instead of single words, and cases are not lacking in which whole sentences are so grasped by a single effort of attention. Other cases, more rare of course, are those in which entire paragraphs, and even a page of a book, are so grasped in a glance by the trained perception. Natural faculty! you may say. Yes! to any extent—but you, yourself, may develop it if you are willing to pay the price of interest, patience, perseverance, work and time.

Sound-Perception

Sound-perception is likewise capable of being trained and developed to the same remarkable degree. In fact, it is so developed in many cases, as we may plainly see by observing those whose occupations require such a keen perception of sound. The cases of skilled musicians occur to you at once in this connection. The average musician detects shades of tone which do not exist for you. The leaders of large orchestras are able to distinguish the slightest error in note or tone of any one of the instruments being played before them—to pick out the softest note in the flute, from the tremendous volume of sound omitted from hundreds of instruments, large and small, is no slight task, yet it is performed daily, many times each day, by the leaders of large orchestras, as any musician will inform you.

There are many persons who are said never to forget a voice they have ever heard; and to be able to distinguish one particular note from any of the thousands of others they may remember. I have known persons to be able to distinguish between footsteps of many persons, coming and going, in the halls of a large institution, simply by sound, the passing persons being out of sight. Telegraphers can tell who is at the other end of the wire, by perceiving slight differences in the sound of the receiving instrument. Machinists can tell in a moment that there is trouble with their particular machine, simply by an almost imperceptible change in the "whir" thereof. Likewise an old engineer will detect and locate engine trouble almost instantly by means of the slight alteration in the nature of the sound reaching his cars. It is said that an old locomotive driver, or engineer, will hear the little scratching sound of the smallest part of his engine, which sound reaches his perception over and above the roar of the running train. Trainmen will tap the wheels of railway carriages, and will know at once if there is a crack or break or other trouble in or about the wheel. Pilots and officers of boats are able to recognize the whistle of any other boat with which they are familiar, and many railroad men are able to recognize the note of different locomotives in the same way.

Touch-Perception

It is well known that many persons have developed the sense of touch to a remarkable degree. We will pass over the wonderful instances of this class of perception on the part of blind persons, although even these properly come under the general rule. Persons who handle certain kinds of merchandise are able to recognize fine points of difference in their wares, simply by touch-perception. Wool sorters, and graders of different kinds of material, have this form of perception highly developed. There are but few lines of trade that do not furnish instances of persons becoming very expert in distinguishing the quality of goods simply by the "feel." Some of these men are paid very high salaries by reason of this faculty.

Smell-Perception

In the same way, the perception of smell may be highly developed and trained by constant and continued practice. This is evidenced by the case of the professional perfumers who are able to distinguish between the most delicate shades of odor. The blind also have this form of perception highly developed, and in many cases are able to distinguish between the odor of gloves, and other articles of apparel, belonging to different persons. I have known young children to possess this faculty of perception to a high degree. I need not refer to the power of animals, dogs in particular, who possess this form of perception developed to a high degree.

It is claimed that each and every person has his or her distinctive personal odor or scent, and that the same may be readily detected and identified by the smell- perception of any person having normal organs of smell, providing sufficient practice and training may be given to the task. Savages have a much keener smell-perception than have the individuals of the civilized races—but it is claimed that if a civilized person undertakes the cultivation of this sense, he will excel the savages therein, owing to his higher power of voluntary concentration and his finer discriminative powers. The civilized races, becoming less and less dependent upon the sense of smell in their daily lives, have allowed this class of sense impressions to practically lapse; but, as before said, the dormant faculty may be aroused into efficiency under the power of the will.

Taste-Perception

In the same way, the perception of taste may be highly developed and trained by practice and use. We have but to point to the case of the epicures, who are able to distinguish many points of difference and distinction in food and drink, which are imperceptible to the ordinary individual. Many persons employed in certain trades have their taste-perception highly developed; and their employment rests and depends upon such proficiency. The tea-tasters, and wine-testers, are well-known examples of this class. A skilled tea-taster will be able to tell not only from where a certain sample of tea has come, but he will also be able to determine very closely its market value and quality, simply by allowing a few drops of the brew to pass over his tongue. The wine-tester is able to perform the same office in the case of wines. In the case of taste-perception, however, the smell-perception is usually also involved, as it is very difficult, comparatively, to rely on the taste-perception alone, if the sense of smell be shut off—for the two classes of sense impressions are very closely related to each other.

In all of these cases of highly developed Perception, however, it is the mental faculty which has become especially efficient—not simply the sense organs. The training that will produce similar results is that of the mind alone. Providing that the sense organism is normal, the power of Perception relating to that particular sense may be cultivated, trained, and developed to an almost incredible degree. It is true that the cultivation of any class of sense-perception is usually accompanied by an increase in the physical efficiency of the organ of sense related to that particular class of perceptions. This is caused by the development of increased sensitiveness of the nervous matter of the sense organs, which are thus able to more delicately "sense" the impressions made upon it by the contact of things of the outside world. It is a fact that attention directed to any part of the body tends to develop sensitiveness at that point—and in the case of sense organs, it tends to increase the efficiency thereof. Moreover, by use and active employment, any physical organ tends to increase in efficiency, at least within certain limits. But, first, last, and all the time, it must be remembered that all cultivation, development, training, and improvement of the perceptive faculties must be accomplished by mental culture and training—there is no other way. And such culture and training is possible only through the use and employment of the power of Attention.

The above facts being noted, it will seem that the logical course for us to follow in this matter would be to lay aside for the moment our consideration of the subject of the Development of Perception, so that we may acquaint ourselves with the laws and principles concerned with the faculty of Attention. Having learned these, we may then return to our consideration of the subject of Perception, and learn how to develop the powers thereof.

Attention

Considering how frequently we employ the term "Attention," and its importance in our mental processes and their resulting action, it is strange how little thought we have given to the question: "What is Attention." While the present work is concerned more particularly with the subject of how to use the Attention, yet we may well spend a moment to consider just what is known regarding the nature of Attention, and the important part it plays in all of our mental life and activity.

The term "Attention" is derived from the Latin term "attendere," meaning "to stretch or bend forward"; the original implication being that in the act of Attention one's mind was extended, stretched out, or bent toward the object of Attention, just as one needs or stretches his neck forward when he wishes to see or hear more effectively. When we "attend" to a thing, we turn our thought or mind toward it by a positive act of the will; in many cases we also make a positive effort to hold the thought or mind on the thing, after having extended it toward it.

Attention is defined by the dictionaries as: "The application of the mind to any object of sense, representation, or thought; the concentration of the mind on any object of sense, or on any mental conception." The more technical definition may be summed up as: "Concentrated Consciousness," for in all acts of Attention there is always a manifestation of concentration. As a leading psychologist has well said: "Attention is consciousness, and something more. It is consciousness voluntarily applied to some determinate object. It is consciousness concentrated." In this last statement is found the explanation of the office of Attention—of the part played by it in the mental processes. The office of Attention may be stated as: The office of concentrating, focusing, or centering consciousness to a focal point of activity. And what is the particular act in which Attention manifests this concentration upon a focal point? Simply the act of Perception which we considered in the preceding chapter. The perceptive power of the mind depends primarily upon the Power of Attention.

And here let us consider an interesting and important point, namely: Attention is not an enlargement or increase in consciousness, but rather a narrowing, condensing, or limiting of consciousness. The act of Attention may be said to consist of three phases, viz.: (1) The earnest fixing of the mind upon some particular object; (2) the persistent holding of the mind upon that object; and (3) the determined shutting-out of the mind (for the time being) of the perception of any other objects struggling for conscious recognition and attention.

It is an axiom of psychology that the degree of concentration or Attention is proportionate to the smallness of the field upon which it is directed. That is to say, the smaller the number of objects that we "pay attention to" at any one time, the greater the degree of Attention such objects will receive. Conversely, the greater the number of such objects, the less the degree. Again, if we concentrate upon a single, simple thing, our perceptive impressions concerning it will be quite distinct, intense, vivid and clear. The increase of the number or degree of complexity of this object results in less clear, less distinct, less intense impressions—unless we attend to it in detail, by mentally breaking it up into small parts, which also proves the rule.

The importance of Attention in the mental processes may be realized by the consideration of the following quotations from eminent psychologists:

"An act of Attention, that is an act of concentration, seems necessary to every exertion of consciousness, as a certain contraction of the pupil is requisite to every exertion of vision. Attention, then, is to consciousness what the contraction of the pupil is to sight; or to the eye of the mind what the microscope or telescope is to the bodily eye. Attention constitutes the better half of all intellectual power." "It is Attention, much more than any difference in the abstract power of reasoning, which constitutes the vast difference which exists between minds of different individuals." "The most important intellectual habit that I know of is the habit of attending exclusively to the matter in hand. It is commonly said that genius cannot be infused by education, yet this power of concentrated Attention, which belongs as a part of his gift to every great discoverer, is unquestionably capable of almost indefinite augmentation by resolute practice." "The force wherewith anything strikes the mind is generally in proportion to the degree of Attention bestowed upon it." "The more completely the mental energy can be brought into one focus, and all distracting objects excluded, by the act of Attention, the more powerful will be the volitional effort."

A leading psychologist has pointed out to his students a very important fact, and at the same time has given a very useful hint, when he says: "There is a constant struggle on the part of sensations to survive in consciousness. The sensation which we allow to take the most forcible hold on the Attention usually wins the day. If we sit by an open window in the country on a summer day, we may have many stimuli knocking at the gate of Attention: the ticking of a clock, the barking of dogs, the lowing of cows, the cries of children at play, the rustling of leaves, the songs of birds, the rumbling of wagons, etc. If Attention is centered upon any one of these, that one for the time being acquires the importance of a king upon the throne of our mental world. But none of these may sway our thoughts, for our Attention may be forcibly directed to some other object, which colors our conscious mental life. Hence it is of the utmost importance for our mental welfare to guard the gates of Attention. Some persons have the power of voluntary Attention developed in such slight degree, that it has been well said that they belong less to themselves than to any object that happens to strike their attention.

There are two phases of Attention: (1) reflex, and (2) voluntary attention. Reflex Attention is drawn from us by a nervous response to some stimulus. Voluntary Attention is given by us to some object of our own selection, and is accompanied by a peculiar sense of effort. Many persons scarcely get beyond the reflex stage. Any chance stimulus will take their attention away from their studies or their business." In what is called Reflex or Involuntary Attention, there is but a slight employment of the will, the process being almost automatic. The child, or person of uncultivated mentality, manifests this form of Attention almost exclusively. Such persons are attracted only by the passing, changing things of the moment, in which the Attention is caught by the outside stimulus easily and almost without the conscious action of the will. It is this form of Attention that we find in the case of children, the lower animals, and in persons of untrained intellect. Wave a stick in front of a dog, or a ball of worsted before a young cat, and the Attention is caught at once. In the same way, the Attention of the child or undeveloped adult is attracted by some similar trifling thing. Such forms of Attention are almost automatic, and belong to the general category of reflex actions of the nervous system, rather than to the class of voluntary actions of the mind. Attention of this class is accompanied by but a minimum of concentration, and an even less degree of detention in consciousness.

In Voluntary Attention, on the other hand, a distinct and deliberate effort of the will is employed, both in the focusing and in the detention in consciousness of the impression. In involuntary, or reflex Attention there is no selection of the object on our part, it being presented from the outside world to our nervous system. But in voluntary Attention we make a deliberate selection of the object to which we wish our mind to attend. Again, in involuntary Attention there is no sense of effort; while in voluntary Attention there is always a peculiar sense of effort, sometimes to a very marked degree. In involuntary Attention there is but a small degree of detention, and even the slightest new stimulus will draw away the Attention from the first object. In voluntary Attention, however, the will holds the Attention to the object before it, and often closes the door of the mind to even marked stimuli from the outside.

The actual experience of every reader of this book will furnish proof of the correctness of the distinction made above between the manifestation of involuntary, or reflex, Attention, and that of voluntary Attention, respectively. It will be found that when the Attention is not specially directed or concentrated upon any one thing, by means of a voluntary effort, the person is more or less conscious of a number of impressions pouring in upon the mind through the channel of the senses. One then sees a number of things, and hears as many more, and may even at the same time receive impressions through the respective senses of taste and smell, and sometimes even the sense of touch may assert itself at the same time. In such cases the Attention may dance backward and forward, here and there, with great rapidity, and the consciousness may receive many impressions with more or less distinctness.

But, let voluntary Attention once concentrate itself upon any given thing, or set of things, and a far different state of affairs if manifested. For instance, a person concentrating his attention upon an interesting book may fail to hear his name called by one of his family, or even to respond to a touch of the hand on the shoulder. He will not hear the doorbell ring, nor perceive the sound of the striking of the passing hour by the clock near to him. The enamored lover is often almost entirely oblivious of the persons and scenes around him, and recalls nothing of them afterward. His attention is concentrated keenly upon the beloved one, and to the rest of the world of impressions he is practically in a trance. Nearly everyone reading the above will be able to corroborate the statements made therein by reason of his or her own experience.

It is related of a well known philosopher that he was so busily occupied in writing one of his books that he failed to hear the voice of the bombardment of the college town by the guns of Napoleon's army; and that he became aware of the fact only when he was brought back to the consciousness of his immediate surroundings by a rough shake of the shoulder at the hands of a grenadier who had penetrated into his study. It is recorded in a number of cases that persons having become intensely interested in some one subject, or sight, have failed to feel pin-pricks or even more severe pain. The story is told of a well known American statesman that he once requested a fellow-congressman to stop him after he had spoken for two hours. But the statesman had been so deeply concentrated upon the subject of his speech, and the delivery thereof, that he failed to be aroused even when his friend repeatedly pricked him in the leg with the point of a pin. Soldiers in battle have failed to perceive pain, owing to their attention having been fixed on the object of the military movement in which they were engaged. Workmen closely interested in their work often fail to hear or see things which are occurring in their near vicinity. In the same way, one often falls into a reverie, or "brown study" in which the outside world is practically shut out. Criminals know that when a crowd is intently watching some interesting sight the persons composing the crowd are far less likely to detect the movements of the pickpockets.

As a rule, the greater the degree of voluntary

Attention given to a special object, the greater will be the degree, and the variety, of conscious impressions from the general environment. The act of concentrated voluntary Attention also tends to magnify the power of the impressions received at the time. If the attention be voluntarily concentrated upon the ticking of a clock, or the dropping of water from a faucet, the sound will often become so intense as to be actually painful. A tiny itching of the skin will have a similar effect under the same circumstances. The buzzing of a mosquito may become maddening, unless the Attention is fixed upon some other object. Consequently, it follows that concentrated voluntary Attention will develop the power of any sense-impression to which it may be directed. In this way we manage to see small objects which were at first invisible to us; or to hear sounds which at first were indistinct. The principle is akin to that of the principle of focus in the sun-glass. It causes the full power of consciousness to be brought to a focal point, by concentrated voluntary Attention, and its power is seemingly magnified in this way.

The power of voluntary Attention varies greatly among different individuals. It may be greatly increased and developed by training and exorcise, however. In fact, the difference between individuals in this respect seems to be almost entirely a matter of exercise, cultivation, and development. Many instances of remarkable development along these lines have been noted in the history of applied psychology. Some eminent authorities, as we have seen in the preceding pages, have gone so far as to say that a highly developed power of concentrated voluntary Attention is the key to much of that which we usually tail "genius"; or, at the least, that it enables its fortunate possessor to duplicate many of the achievements of genius. It is conceded by the best psychologists that voluntary Attention is one of the highest forms or phases of mental activity, and is found to be largely developed in the case of all men of great intellectual power. The same authorities tell us that imbeciles, and persons of weak intellectual powers, have little or no power of concentrated voluntary Attention. Voluntary Attention, that is Attention directed, concentrated, and maintained by a special act of the will, is the mark of the trained intellect, and is the badge of developed mental efficiency in any line of human endeavor. It is one of the special characteristics of the Master Mind.

A leading psychologist says: "The first step toward the development of the will lies in the exercise of Attention. There is a sense of conscious effort in voluntary Attention. This suffices to mark it off from the involuntary type. When there is a flash of lightning, we attend involuntarily; when we look into a microscope to discriminate between the atoms seen floating there, we put voluntary effort into our Attention. Ideas grow in distinctness and in motor power as we attend to them. If we take two ideas of the same intensity, and center the attention upon one, we shall notice how much it grows in power. Take the sensations from two aches in the body, and fix Attention upon the one. That idea will grow in motor power until we may act in a direction supposed to relieve that particular pain, while the other is comparatively neglected. If we, at the start, want several things in about an equal degree, whether a bicycle, a typewriter, or a encyclopedia, we shall end by wanting that one the most on which our attention has been most strongly centered. The bicycle idea may thus gain more motor power than either of the other two; or, if we keep thinking how useful a encyclopedia would be, action may tend in that direction. There is no dispute over the fact that voluntary Attention is the most important element in will. In order to act in the direction of one idea in preference, to another, we must dismiss the one and voluntarily attend to the other. The motor force thus developed in connection with the dominant idea lies at the foundation of every higher act of will."

The same authority also says: "When it is said that Attention will not take hold on an uninteresting object, we must not forget that anyone not shallow and fickle can soon discover something interesting in most objects. Here cultivated minds show their especial superiority, for the Attention which they are able to give generally ends in finding a pearl in the most uninteresting looking oyster. When an object necessarily loses interest from one point of view, such minds discover in it new attributes The essence of genius is to present an old thing in new ways, whether it be some force in nature or some aspect in humanity."

From what has been said concerning the nature and power of voluntary Attention, and from what will be said from time to time on the same subject as we proceed with our study of the general subject of the Master Mind in the pages of this book, the reader will see that the weapon of voluntary Attention is the most efficient in the collection of the mental weapons in the armory of the Master Mind. It is by means of the power of voluntary Attention that the Ego really brings into subjection and obedience the various faculties and forces of the mind, which without it often tend to become rebellious and disobedient.

The Ego, controlling the power of voluntary Attention is able not only to select the nature and character of his thoughts, and to cause his mind to think intelligently and efficiently, but it also is able to control the feelings and desires which serve as the usual motive of will-action. As we proceed, we shall see that the Ego is able to change the desire to act this way or that way into the desire to act some other way, and to set the activity of will flowing along the particular channels chosen freely by itself. As we have said elsewhere, the Ego, in such cases, is able to "will to will," instead of being carried along in the current of some "desire to will." The Ego is the King of His Throne—and Voluntary Attention is his Sword of Power.

The Mastery of Perception

A leading psychologist has given us perhaps the most comprehensive, and at the same time the most condensed, statement of the Laws of Attention to be found in any of the text books, which statement is as follows:

"(1) Attention will not attach itself to uninteresting things. (2) It will soon decline in vigor (a) if the stimulus is unvarying, or (b) if some new attribute is not discovered in the object. (3) Attention cannot remain constant in the same direction for a long period, because (a) the nervous apparatus of the senses soon tire under the strain of continuous attention toward any one object, and consequently respond with less vigor, (b) the same is true of brain cells. To prove the truth of this one has only to focus the eye continuously on one object, or to keep the attention fixed on the same phase of a subject. (4) When one kind of attention is exhausted, we may rest ourselves in two ways: (a) by giving ourselves up to the play of reflex (involuntary) attention, or (b) by directing our voluntary attention into a new channel. The amount of fatigue must determine which is better. (5) Attention too continuously centered upon the same unvarying sensation, or upon any unchanging object, has been proved by experiment to tend

122

to induce either the hypnotic state or a coma-
tose condition."

The secret of developing the power of Perception through the efficient employment of the
Power of Attention consists in the main in the
intelligent practice of the principles announced
in the above quoted statement of the Laws of
Attention. This being so, it follows that, at the
very start of our consideration of the subject
of The Mastery of Perception, we should fully
acquaint ourselves with the merit and meaning
of the said principles, that we may efficiently
employ the same in our work of the Mastery of
Perception. The following suggestions may be
found of interest and value in this connection:

The first of the above laws states the difficulty
of attaching the Attention to uninteresting
things. But there is a remedy for this as follows: (a) in the application of the equally true
principle that interest may be developed in a
previously uninteresting thing, by studying and
analyzing it. Everything has its interesting side,
and examination will bring this into view, (b)
By viewing a thing from varying viewpoints,
and from different angles of physical and mental vision, new facts are discovered regarding
it, and these discoveries awaken interest and
renewed Attention.

The same remedy applies in the case of the second law. For by changing the point of view, and by discovering new qualities, properties and attributes in a thing, the stimulus is varied, and renewed interest is obtained.

The third law explains why the Attention cannot long remain focused in the same direction. A remedy for this will be found in the well-known psychological rule to study a thing by piecemeal. That is to say, instead of considering attentively the entire subject, or object, one should break it (mentally) into as many small sections as possible, and then proceed to study it by sections, one after another. This will vary the stimulus, increase interest, and widen the inquiry by reason of the analytical treatment. Remember that we learned the alphabet letter by letter, and not as a whole learned at one effort of the mind. This is not only the easiest way to "know" a subject, but it is also the best way to acquire a thorough knowledge of any subject or object.

The fourth law informs us that we may obtain rest for the tired Attention by (a) relaxing the voluntary Attention, and opening our consciousness to the impressions of involuntary, or reflex Attention—paying attention to the sights and sounds reaching us from outside, as for instance by closing our book and looking out of the window at the passing persons and things; or (b) by directing our voluntary Attention into a new channel, as by closing our book and picking up and reading another book along entirely different lines; or changing from an abstract subject to a concrete proposition, or vice versa. This expresses an important psychological principle, i.e., that the best way to rest and relax the Attention is to change the direction of its effort and activity. Change of occupation gives the best kind of rest to physical or mental muscles. Using one set of muscles, or brain-cells, gives the other set a chance to rest and recuperate. Some of our deepest thinkers have applied this principle by occasionally laying aside the important subjects of their thought, and then resting the minds by reading a thrilling and exciting, though trashy, detective story.

The fifth law merely serves to emphasize the effect of the unnatural concentration of Attention; and the fact that a varying stimulus is necessary for continued consciousness. It serves to point us to the middle of the road, avoiding the extreme of undue concentration on a single object on the one hand, and the other extreme of bestowing no voluntary Attention at all.

By acquainting himself with the general principles underlying the subject of Attention, as above given and commented upon, the reader will be better prepared to understand and assimilate the many applications of the said principles, under many and varying forms of application, in our further consideration of the subject of the Mastery of Perception. In our consideration of the above quoted Laws of Attention, we saw that the Attention would not easily attach itself to uninteresting things; and that the only way to overcome this trait was to make interesting the object which we wished to examine carefully under concentrated voluntary Attention. This, fortunately for us, is made possible to us by reason of the psychological law that "interest is awakened by Attention," which is just as true as that "Attention follows interest." The average person is able to arouse and maintain Attention only when interest already attaches to the object to be considered. But the Master Mind rides over this obstacle by first awakening interest in the thing by means of a careful examination under concentrated voluntary Attention, and thereafter allowing the Attention to flow freely along the channels of interest thus made. Here we have an instance of the will first creating a channel, and then traveling over its course.

In connection with the above, a leading psychologist has said: "When it is said that attention will not take a firm hold on an uninteresting thing, we must not forget that anyone not shallow and fickle can soon discover something interesting in most objects. Here cultivated minds show their especial superiority, for the attention which they are able to give generally ends in finding a pearl in the most uninteresting oyster. When an object necessarily loses interest from one point of view, such minds discover it in new attributes. The essence of genius is to present an old thing in new ways, whether it be some force in nature or some aspect of humanity."

In short, if the subject which you wish to master, or the object with which you wish to become thoroughly acquainted, seems at first to be uninteresting, then your first task is to convert that uninteresting thing into an interesting one by discovering the interesting traits about it—and such traits are always there. A writer has said about Agassiz, the great scientist, and his work: "A grasshopper is to most persons an oblong insect, capable of jumping. Agassiz's pupils say that after he had compelled them to find out a world of interesting matter about it, they would sometimes go to hear him deliver a popular lecture. They noticed that the audience became as much interested in the grasshopper as if he were reading from a romance." Those who have read Fabre's several works on insect life, in which he describes the respective lives of the bee, the ant, the spider, etc., will readily understand how extreme interest may be created in a commonplace subject, or a commonplace object, by means of a masterful examination of the subject or subject in question.

The allusion to Agassiz naturally brings to mind the well-known story of how he once taught a new pupil how to perceive—and how to discover interesting facts in an uninteresting object. Agassiz, as you probably know, was renowned not only for his own remarkable powers of perception, but also for the fact that he developed like powers in his pupils—and that therefore his services as a teacher were in great demand. The following story contains a powerful lesson, and the reader is asked to carefully consider it.

Here is the story in question: A pupil appeared before the great teacher for instruction. The teacher took the pupil into the laboratory, and there laid out a fish before him, telling him to closely examine the outer appearance thereof, and to prepare himself to make a full report about it when asked. The teacher then left the room, leaving the pupil alone with the fish. He looked the fish over for a few minutes, noting its general shape, its fins, its tail, etc., and was sure that he had learned all that was to be known of the outer form of that fish at the end of a quarter-hour. He then grew tired of waiting for the teacher who had disappeared. In disgust, he again seated himself before the fish, and looked casually at it— and lo! he saw something new in its details. Becoming then interested in spite of himself, he examined it still more carefully and in closer detail, and was amazed to discover quite a number of new details.

Then came another period of disgusted waiting. He knew all about that fish (so he thought), and why should he be kept waiting longer? Lunch time came—and still no teacher. After eating his lunch, he returned to the old fish in order to kill time. He began idly to count its scales, and in doing so was surprised to notice that the fish was without eyelids. Then the teacher returned, and expressed dissatisfaction with the results of the observation of the pupil. He again left the latter alone with the fish, telling him in parting that "a pencil is the best of eyes," and bidding him note on paper the results of his further observations as he proceeded. The student, in despair, plunged again into the task. And lo! as he discovered point after point of new details about the fish, he began to find a new interest awakening. And before long he was amazed at the long list of new points that he had discovered and noted down.

Agassiz kept the young man at work on this fish for three long days, and was rewarded by securing a remarkably long list of details that the pupil had observed and discovered. But best of all—and this was the real purpose and intent of the lesson— the student had acquired the knowledge that a careful examination of an uninteresting subject tended to develop a live and active interest therein, which interest then tended to spur on the Attention to further acts of Perception.

The thoughtful reader will probably have already noted that in the above story is also contained the lesson of overcoming the obstacles mentioned in our presentation of the second law of Attention, i.e., the fact that the Attention will decline in vigor if (a) the stimulus is unvarying, or (b) of some new attribute is not discovered in the object. In the case of Agassiz's pupil it will be noted that "the stimulus was unvarying" after he had exhausted his discovery of the most superficial facts concerning the fish, and that thereafter his Attention waned and he became wearied, bored, and disgusted. When, later, he made the discovery of "new attributes," he awakened his "second wind" of interest and Attention. And so he proceeded, each new set of discoveries serving to renew his interest and the vigor of his Attention. And each new set of discoveries tended to rest certain brain cells concerned in the discovery of previous attributes of the fish. The "something new" in the fish tended to not only arouse fresh interest and mental vigor, but also to rest his mind. There is a great lesson here for those who can understand it.

The reader who may wish to practice exercises tending to develop his or her powers of Perception may easily arrange such exercises for himself, or herself, by basing the exercises upon the above recorded story of Agassiz and his pupil. Many teachers give quite a number of such exercises, but an analysis thereof will show that the principle underlying all of them is practically the same. This principle is simple: it consists merely in placing an object before you, and then studying all of its details, making a list of the same in writing as you proceed. Note the general shape of the object, its color, etc., and then proceed to an examination and analysis of its minor details. By so doing you will finally build a general chart of the thing, with general divisions and details under each class. When your interest wanes, rest your mind by putting the object away from you find turning your attention to other things—less serious things, in fact.

Then, the following day, resume the task by trying to recall as many of the previously recorded points as possible, and then read over your list and see how many you have missed. Then start afresh with your investigations. You will be surprised to discover how fresh your interest has again become for the task. You will then discover may new details. Repeat this exercise on the same object for several days, until you are satisfied that you have exhausted its possibilities. Each time you take it up you will discover new details, and will awaken a fresh interest. And, at the same time you will be pleased to discover that your general powers of Perception have increased to a marked degree.

After having mastered the principle of the said class of exercises, you may proceed to a more complex phase. This new phase consists in quickening the power of Perception in the perception of a number of articles at the same time. A favorite exercise of certain schools of mental training is that which develops the power of the person so instantaneously add up a number of small objects, marbles or beans for instance. In practicing this exercise, begin with a small number, and then add one or two to the number each day—picking up the pile without knowing the exact number, of course, and then after taking a hasty glance at the pile try to state the exact number thereof. A variation of this is had in the familiar trick of bookkeepers of adding several figures at one mental operation—beginning with groups of two, and then increasing the number from time to time.

Another form of this exercise is what is known as "The Houdini Exercise" which, by the way, is the method employed by Houdini whereby he acquired the faculty of passing by a large shop window and "taking in" all the articles contained therein at a single comprehensive glance. Houdini began training for this feat by the preliminary practice of laying a number of dominoes before him, spread out on the table, face up; he took a hasty but keen glance at the dominoes, and then wrote down what he had observed. He soon was able to set down the names of quite a large number of dominoes—but he had first built up the power of persistent and determined practice and exercise.

In France, and in Italy, the schoolboys play a game which is based on precisely the same principle as that just stated. The Italian boys are very proficient at this game, which they call "Morro," while the French boys call it "little foxes"—and its practice does indeed make little foxes of them. The game consists of one boy showing a closed fist from which he suddenly extends several fingers. The other boy must state instantly, and without hesitation, the exact number of fingers shown. The best guesser wins the game. A variation of the game consists in the quick statement of a number of small beans shown in a suddenly opened hand. It is amazing what a degree of proficiency is attained by these little games. And it cannot be doubted that the proficiency thus gained is of value to them in their after life, for it certainly increases the power of Perception along certain lines.

A leading psychologist says, regarding this point of practice and its results: "Criminals have some excellent methods for training the young. An instructor in the department of thievery will place on the palm of his hand a number of objects, say a coin, a chestnut, a button, a key, a bean. He will unclasp his hand for a second before a number of boys, who are expected not only to name all the objects, but to describe them. For instance, the value of the coin must be given, and the shape of the key accurately described, or drawn on paper or in the dirt. Then the instructor will, perhaps, substitute a hazelnut for the chestnut and a pea for the bean, but woe to the boy who does not instantaneously detect the difference. These boys are sent out for the feigned purpose of begging. They catch a glimpse of the parlor, the hall, the kitchen, or the office, and in that one glance they note the position and value of everything. They then report to the men who sent them out, and a burglary is planned. It is a pity that such excellent methods of teaching rapidity of Perception are, for the most part, left to criminals."

The same writer says; "Successful gamblers often become so expert in noticing the slightest change of an opponent's facial expression that they will estimate the strength of his hand by the involuntary signs which appear in the face and which are frequently checked the instant they appear. There are many excellent methods for cultivating rapidity of Perception, and they can be employed with but little trouble. At the start, place upon a small table seven different articles. Remove for an instant the cloth used to cover them, and then have some one describe the articles. This can be played as a game, and prizes are offered to the one naming the most things. Only one should be allowed to approach the table at once, and the cloth should be raised for the same length of time for each one. To avoid disputes, each one should at once sit down in another room, or in a different part of the same room, the name of each article seen.

The number of things on the table should be gradually increased to forty. If different things are at the same time tossed into the air and allowed to fall behind a screen, or into a basket, bag, or sheet gathered up, great quickness of Perception will be necessary to name and describe all.

Extreme rapidity of perception, due to careful training, was one of the factors enabling Houdini and his son to astonish everybody and to make a fortune. He placed a domino before the boy, and instead of allowing him to count the spots, required him to give the sum total at once. This exercise was continued until each could give instantaneously the sum of spots on a dozen dominoes. The sum was given just as accurately as if five minutes had been consumed in adding."

In Oriental lands there is frequently played a series of games which really are carefully designed exercises calculated to develop to a high degree the power of quickness and accuracy of perception among the young. Many Orientals are able to cast a single, apparently sleepy, casual glance at a table full of objects, and then to write down a full and complete list thereof. This power is not a natural gift, as many suppose when witnessing these feats, but is rather entirely a matter of hard work, careful training from childhood, and steady practice. A typical instance of this form of Perception-training is related by Kipling in his interesting tale of his little hero, "Kim," in his story of that name. This tale, somewhat abbreviated is given below, and is worthy of careful consideration and analysis, for it teaches an important lesson along the very lines which we are now considering. Here follows the synopsis of the incident:

Kim was matched against a native boy, by old Lurgan Sahib, who wished to train Kim for the Indian Secret Service work, in which accurate and rapid perception is most essential. The native boy was an old hand at the game, while Kim was a novice. The old man threw fifteen jewels on a tray, and bade the two boys gaze upon them for a moment or two. Then the tray was covered, and each boy recited what he had observed. Here follows the result, in the words of Kipling: " 'There are under that paper five blue stones, one big, one smaller, and three small,' said Kim all in haste. 'There are four green stones, and one with a hole in it; there is one yellow stone that I can see through, and one like a pipe stem. There are two red stones, and—and—I have made the count fifteen, but two I have forgotten. No! give me time. One was of ivory, little and brownish, and—and—

137

give me time.' But Kim could do no better. 'Hear my count,' cried the native child. 'First are two flawed sapphires, one of two ruttees and one of four, as I should judge. The four ruttee sapphire is chipped at the edge. There is one Turkestan turquoise, plain with green veins, and there are two inscribed—one with the name of God in gilt, and the other being cracked across, for it came out of an old ring, I cannot read. We have now five blue stones; four flamed emeralds there are, but one is drilled in two places, and one is a little carven.' 'Their weight!' said Lurgan Sahib, impassively. 'Three—five—and four ruttees, as I judge it. There is one piece of greenish amber, and a cheap cut topaz from Europe. There is one ruby of Burma, one or two ruttees, without a flaw. And there is a ballas ruby, flawed, of two ruttees. There is a carved ivory from China, representing a rat sucking an egg; and there is last—Ah, ha!—a ball of crystal as big as a bean, set in gold leaf.' He clapped his hands at the close."

It may interest the reader to know that the mortified, defeated Kim so profited by the experience that he managed, finally, to outdo the native boy at his own game, and by so doing aroused the jealousy of the latter to such an extent that he tried to murder Kim. It may also interest the reader to hear the final advice to Kim, regarding these exercises, given by old Lurgan Sahib, as follows: "The secret consists in doing it many times over, till it is done perfectly, for it is worth doing."

Of interest, and undoubted value also, to the student of this subject of the Mastery of Perception, is the quotation from Maupassant, the great French writer, in which he tells the story of how his master, Flaubert (another great French writer), taught him how to be original in literary expression. It will be seen at once that the method both requires, and at the same time develops, keenness, accuracy, and rapidity of Perception. Flaubert told Maupassant: "Talent is nothing but long patience. Go to work! Everything which one desires to express must be looked at with sufficient attention, and during a sufficiently long time, to discover in it some aspect which no one has yet seen or described. In everything there is still some spot unexplored, because we are accustomed only to use our eyes with the recollection of what others before us have thought on the subject which we contemplate. The smallest object contains something unknown. Find it! To describe a fire that flames, and a tree on a plain, look, keep looking, at that flame and that tree until in your eyes they have lost all resemblance to any other tree or any other fire. That is the way to become original."

Maupassant adds: "Having laid down this truth, that there are not in the whole world two grains of sand, two specks, two hands, or two noses exactly alike, Flaubert compelled me to describe in a few phrases a being or an object in such a manner as to distinguish it from all other objects of the same race or the same species. "When you pass a grocer seated at his shop door, a janitor smoking his pipe, a stand of hackney coaches, show me that grocer and that janitor—their attitude, their whole physical appearance—embracing, likewise, as indicated by the skillfulness of the picture, their whole moral nature; so that I cannot confound them with any other grocer, or any other janitor. Make me see, in one word, that a certain cab horse does not resemble the fifty others that follow or precede it."

There is contained in the above quotation from Maupassant the essence of the entire philosophy of efficient observation and trained perceptive powers. Study it carefully, with concentrated attention and interest, so as to grasp the principle clearly. Can you doubt the degree of perceptive power necessary to fulfill the requirements therein stated? Can you doubt that the impressions arising from such an exercise of perceptive power would be clear cut and distinct, and all-embracing? And can you doubt the result of even a reasonable degree and amount of practice along the lines indicated?

Exercises in Perception

The student who will master the principles underlying the incidents related in detail in the preceding chapter should be able to invent, and to prescribe, exercises in perceptive efficiency for himself; for the principles are so general and universal that a wealth of practical forms of applying them will be thought of by the student possessing the constructive imagination.

But, inasmuch, as many persons prefer to be positively told "just how," instead of discovering the road for themselves after the general direction has been pointed out to them, we have thought it well to insert here a number of detailed exercises, and additional rules, for the practice of the student. These exercises and rules are chiefly compiled from the work on "Memory Training," written by the writer of the present book, but are, of course, adapted and arranged for the special purpose now before us in the present book. It may be mentioned, in this connection, that as the strength of an impression upon the memory depends materially upon the degree of perceptive power and energy bestowed upon the impression, therefore the subject of Efficient Perception is very closely bound up with that of Efficient Memory; and that whatever tends to promote one of these, will necessarily tend to promote the other.

Exercise. Enter a room, and take a careful look around you, endeavoring to perceive and observe as many things as possible that are contained therein. Then leave the room, and write down a list of what you have remembered. After a time, return to the room, and compare your list with the articles actually in the room. Then go out of the room, and make up a second list, including the old as well as the new things observed. Repeat this a number of times, taking care, always, not to fatigue yourself—take time to rest yourself at any stage of the exercise. As you progress, note not only the articles in the room, but also the shape, size, and general form of the room; the location of doors and windows; the location of pictures and decorations; the wallpaper, window shades, fireplace, etc. In short, persevere until you can furnish a complete diagram of the room, as well as a complete list and description of its contents. Try this experiment in your own room, if you like; by so doing you will discover how little you really know about its real appearance or contents. Get acquainted with your room, and at the same time develop your power of Perception, and your memory—for that will be the actual result.

Exercise. Walk along the street, and observe

closely some building which you pass— a house, or shop, or your own residence, for that matter. Then return to your room and note carefully on paper all that you have observed about that building. Then, later on, return to the building and make a comparison with your list. Then make a new list, including old and new points discovered, and so on as we have directed in the preceding exercise. In this and similar exercises you will find it advisable and helpful to proceed from simple to complex—from general aspects to details. You will also find it a great aid to classify as you proceed, making groups and classes of observed details and points. For instance, first take in the general appearance of the building, its size, shape, and form. Then regard its general color-scheme, etc. Then take note of its doors, its windows, working down to greater and greater degree of detail, and to smaller classes, as you proceed. In short, proceed to analyze your object, and then build it up as a whole from your analysis. After you have finished your consideration of one building, take up the one next to it, and so on, until you can correctly describe every building on the block. Or, if you like, confine yourself to corner buildings, and thus make a mental geography of any street or locality you may select.

You will be surprised to see how rapidly you

will acquire efficient Perception in this work. After a time you will become able to "size up" a building fairly well at a single glance, and almost unconsciously. In fact, many builders, architects, and others interested in buildings, do this very thing from acquired habit, and without conscious intention. Likewise, the shoemaker generally takes a hasty glance at the feet of the passers-by, without consciously realizing just what he is doing, but nevertheless taking full notes of anything and everything of importance concerning your footgear. The hatter does the same thing in relation to the headgear of the passers-by. The explanation, of course, lies in the fact of interest-attention and attention-interest, manifesting in Perception directed toward objects connected with the observer's general or particular interest. It is safe to say that you, yourself, already have acquired this habit of observation concerning the things most intimately connected with your business or professional interests, or your particular trade or occupation. The things which bring you a profit, in money or in pleasure, invariably hold your interest, and therefore attract your attention, and thus cause you to manifest more or less efficient Perception concerning them.

The study of faces is an excellent training and exercise for the development of effective Perception. The study of the general outward characteristics of persons, their manner of walking, speaking, etc., as well as their clothing, will be found to be excellent material for exercises of this kind, and will besides be of practical value to you in your ordinary everyday business or professional life in which you meet different persons.

Ear Perception. As the majority of perceptive impressions are received through the channel of the eye, it is natural to devote more time and space to a consideration of visual perception. But we must not neglect the second great channel of impressions— the channel of the ear. The same principle of mastery and development hold good here also. Some persons have excellent eye-perception but poor ear-perception. Modern teachers note this difference in children, and adapt their instruction accordingly. Many persons manifesting a poor ear-perception are apt to think that they have deficient hearing. In many cases, however, this is a mistake, for their trouble arises simply from a lack of attention and interest—a poor condition of ear- perception naturally follows in the train thereof. Many persons fall into the habit of inattention to what is being said to them, allowing their attention to be caught or held by their visual impressions. This is often excused on the ground of "poor hearing," "slight deafness," etc. Such persons may not perceive ordinary remarks made in a loud tone of voice, but will catch the slightest whisper of others if they think that the others are gossiping about them or whispering a secret withheld from themselves. A person may catch the murmured words of love addressed to himself, or the whispered remark concerning his money affairs, but he still will be "slightly deaf" to ordinary remarks.

A well-known psychologist once said: "It cannot be doubted that fully one-half of the deafness that exists is the result of inattention." And another has said: "What is commonly called deafness is not infrequently to be attributed to inattention—the sounds being heard, but not interpreted or recognized." Sounds may be distinctly heard when the attention is directed toward them, that in ordinary circumstances would be imperceptible; and people often fail to hear what is said to them, because they are not paying attention.

The present writer personally knows a very excellent lady who constantly complains that "something must be the matter with me, for I cannot hear a thing that is told me—my hearing must be failing." But one observing her expression of countenance when she is listening to the whispered secrets of others in her near vicinity can see at once that she is fully cognizant of what is being said. He once played a rather mean trick upon this lady—purely as a matter of scientific interest, however. In the midst of our conversation he interjected a French "nonsense verse," uttered in a monotonous, solemn, emphatic tone—the verse being something like one of "Mother Goose," only if anything still more nonsensical. The good lady, looking at him earnestly, replied: "I perfectly agree with you, Professor; in fact, I have always held precisely the same views." She had not really "heard" a word that had been said. A few moments later, he lowered his voice so that it was little more than a murmur, and, attracting her close attention, told her a little bit of spicy gossip about one of her rivals. She heard every word distinctly, without the slightest trouble, and answered him quite intelligently. It was all a matter of the degree of attention given to the remarks in either ease. We trust that the reader will see the point of this, and will profit by the moral contained therein.

Here is the secret of developing ear-perception, contained in a single sentence: Use your ears—practice, exercise, and observe—with attention-interest and interest- attention. Study tones, expressions of voice, accents, inflections, etc. If you see fit, endeavor to mimic and imitate the peculiarities of vocal expression observed by you (never imitate or mimic a stammerer, though, for this trait is "catching"). Your growing interest in the subject of vocal expression will awaken your perceptive powers of attention, and your Perception will develop as a consequence. Practice in the direction of "picking up" scraps of conversation of passers-by on the street, and afterward repeat them to yourself. Follow the same course in attending lectures, church services, and plays at the theatre—try afterwards to recall the exact words if possible. Listen carefully to what is said to you, with the fixed idea of recalling the exact words afterward. Also study the voices of different persons, so that you can identify an unseen person by his voice previously heard by you.

In all of the foregoing exercises and suggestions, you will notice ever present the one same principle, i.e., the principle of attention-interest, and interest-attention. Add to this exercise and diligent practice, and you will have the whole thing in a nutshell. The very simplicity of the secret causes many to fail to value it properly— but here, as in many other things, the greatest truths are the simplest at the last analysis.

The following general rules, and the comments thereon, regarding the Practice of Perception Development, will he found very useful to the student if carefully studied and the principle thereof grasped.

Rule 1. The value of our idea concerning an object depends materially upon the degree of clearness and strength of our perception of the object.

The student should remember this important rule, for it lies at the very foundation of the subject. The idea concerning an observed object is like the record on a phonographic roll, or upon the photographic film. A faint perceptive-impression can never produce a reproduction clearer than itself. A blurred and indistinct perceptive impression will bring forth a blurred and indistinct idea. Perceptions are the things from which ideas are manufactured. Like produces like.

Rule 2. The depth and clearness of a perceptive-impression is in direct proportion to the interest-attention, and attention-interest, bestowed upon the object or subject producing the impression.

There is no perceptive-impression without attention; and attention depends materially upon the interest in, or liking for, the subject or object producing the impression. It is necessary to cultivate interest in the things which you desire to understand and know. Interest may be stimulated by concentrated voluntary attention. And also by habit. And, also, in a secondary way, by attaching your thought or ideas concerning the thing to that of some other thing which has an interest for you, or to the thought of the pleasant and desirable results to be attained by you as a consequence of your mastery of the subject in question. By connecting the idea of the uninteresting thing with that of an interesting one, a secondary interest attaches to the former.

Rule 3. Build a strong primary foundation perceptive-impression of a thing which you wish to know and understand, upon which you can erect a structure of subsequent perceptive-impressions.

The best psychologists agree that it is of prime importance to build a good, strong, foundation of perceptive-impressions, upon which subsequent impressions may be built into a structure of thought. Add to these primary impressions from time to time. Be careful of your foundation work. Let it be strong and firm. A weak foundation of perceptive impressions has wrecked many a promising thought structure. Build on solid rock, and not upon the shifting sands. Upon the perceptive-impression of the main principles of the thought in question, you can afterward build layer after layer of perceptions concerning the details, incidents, and associated facts concerning the main principle.

Rule 4. Let your primary perceptions consist of the main facts, points, principles, form, and characteristics of the thing observed, avoiding too many unimportant details at that moment.

In acquiring perceptive-impressions of a thing which you wish to understand and know, select the "big facts" for your primary work. Or, changing the figure of speech, you should draw in your mind the broad, wide, outlines of the thing, into which you can fill the little details of subsequent perceptions. In learning about a house, begin with the general outlines and appearance, and then fill in the details of your picture. In studying a tree, first see it as a whole, then study its trunk, then its branches, then its twigs, then its leaves, etc., in natural order. Study the whole family, then the groups thereof, and then the particular individuals. All subjects or objects may be studied in this way, for the principle is capable of universal application.

Rule 5. Classify your perceptions of details into divisions, sub-divisions, and then smaller ones; make your whole impression consist of classified parts; let your unity be composed of units.

This rule embodies a very important law of thought. Knowledge properly classified is available knowledge. An idea, with the details thereof properly classified, is available knowledge. An idea with its details thus classified is not only a strong, well established idea, but one which is valuable for the purpose of being combined with other ideas. Without classification of details, the idea of anything is more or less blurred and indistinct, and cannot be well employed in the office of thought.

Rule 6. A perceptive-impression may be intensified by frequent revival in consciousness.

The above constitutes a very important principle in the cultivation of memory, but it is equally applicable to the processes of perception in general. The principle operates so that when you revive in conscious attention (by recollection) an original perceptive-impression, you actually intensify it in consciousness, and cause it to become deeper and stronger. A little thought will show you that most things that you know well you have learned in obedience to this great law of mental activity. Herein lies the importance of "review work" in one's studies. A familiar application of this principle is found in the well-known illustration of remembering the features of a new acquaintance. It is a fact that even if you spend a full hour with the person at the first interview, you may fail to recognize him the next time you see him, whereas, if you see him twelve days in succession, for only five minutes at a time, you will feel that you know him very well indeed, and will have no trouble in remembering him thereafter. Thus, the frequent revival of the perception of a popular song may tend to become a nuisance in time, for you will know it far too well for comfort.

Rule 7. In reviving perceptive-impressions, do not be content with merely repeating the actual perception of the object itself; but also review and revive the impression in consciousness, without actual perception of the original object.

It is, as has been said, a great benefit to re-examine an object for the purpose of intensifying our original impression of it. In this way the original impression is strengthened, and we also add new details of perceptive impression by this repeated reference to and examination of the object itself. In fact, one may practically educate himself on a subject or object in this

way. But this form of the revival of the perceptive impressions, important as it is, may be
materially reinforced by the simple revival in
consciousness of the original impressions, without a reference to the object itself. By taking
the impression into the field of consciousness,
by the action of the memory, the impression is
given depth and strength which it would otherwise lack. We need not enter into a technical
consideration of the psychological reason for
the fact just stated; it is enough to say that all
psychologists realize that the depth and strength
of a perceptive-impression are greatly added to
by this revival in consciousness without reference to the original object.

We may appreciate the importance of this rule
if we will but turn to some familiar examples
of its employment; therefore, let us take two
familiar examples to illustrate this point. Let
us consider two boys learning the multiplica-
tion table. The first boy refers to the printed
tables whenever he wishes to know how much
is "seven times eight," or "five times six." The
second boy reviews his memorized work, and,
whenever he wishes to know the product of
7x8 or 5x6 he recalls the memorized result and
applies it to the case before him. Or, again, let
us consider the difference between two persons
wishing to spell correctly; one refers to his

dictionary without any attempt to draw on his stored-away impressions concerning the subject, while the second does so draw upon his stored-away impressions, and refers to the book only when he is unable to recall the former. Which class of persons will acquire the deepest and strongest impressions of the particular subjects referred to? Can there he any doubt as to the correct answer?

The best way to intensify a perceptive-impression of any subject or object, under the present rule, is as follows: (1) first revive in consciousness the original impression of the thing, endeavoring to recall everything originally included and contained in that general impression. Then note on paper what you can recall of the original impression. You will discover that the use of the pencil will greatly facilitate your collection of the thing. (2) Then refer once more to the object itself, comparing it with your written list of the incidents of the impression; you will thus discover what you have omitted, and this perception will tend to strengthen and deepen the original one. In doing this you will also probably discover some new items concerning the thing, which will naturally be added to the original general impression.

In the application of this rule will be found the

proof of the old school room adage that "An un-recited lesson is only half learned, and is soon forgotten."

Rule 8. In storing away a perceptive impression, endeavor to link and associate it with as many old impressions as possible, for each link of association is a tie which bind the impression to other items of knowledge concerning the general subject.

We shall defer our comments on this rule until we consider the Principle of Association, in another chapter of this book. We call your attention here, however, to the fact that in forming these associative links and ties you are also "classifying" the impression, as advised in Rule 5.

Rule 9. Strive to impress a perceptive-impression upon the mind through as many channels of sense perception as possible. If you are weak in any particular form of perception, then rivet the impression received through this weak channel by means of another perceptive-impression received through a channel of stronger perception— clinch the weaker by using the stronger in connection with it.

The rule embodies a well-established psychological principle. Common experience proves that in many cases a perceptive impression is greatly intensified if it is built up of perceptions arriving through different sense channels. This is well illustrated by the processes of memorizing certain forms of perceptions. For instance, the majority of persons find it easier to remember names, numbers, etc., if they also are able to see the printed or written word at the same time that they hear the name or number spoken. Many persons have learned the advantage of writing down names, numbers, etc., which they wish to memorize, after having heard them spoken—the written memorandum then being destroyed. There are three senses involved in such a process of impression-storing, viz.: (1) the sense of hearing, (2) the sense of sight, and (3) the sense of muscular motion, which is a form of touch sensation. The first two are familiar to you, but the third is likely rather unfamiliar. But you really receive and store away impressions received through this channel; for instance, we could not write, walk, skate, or use the needle, knife and fork, or the typewriter, did we not acquire and recall impressions through this channel. "We learn to perform motions habitually and almost unconsciously simply by means of the perceptive-impressions received and increased in strength and power by repetition through this channel.

In the same way, it is found to be of advantage to visualize a thing with which you wish to become well acquainted, and to understand and know thoroughly. By creating a mental picture of the object, you will be greatly aided in recalling your perceptive impressions concerning it. The picture recalled in addition to the name of a thing often enables us to think very clearly and efficiently concerning it. In the same way, many have found it of advantage to recall the name or title of an object when they were viewing it through the channel of the sight. If your eye-perception is weak, you may add to the strength of your perceptive-impression concerning a thing by means of repeating to yourself its name or title when you are examining it visually. Even the other senses may be called in operation in this connection, in some cases. For instance, the perceptive-impression of Limburger Cheese certainly is heightened and deepened if the person adds to his sight-impression, and sound-impression of the name, the smell-impression arising from a close contact with it. Or, again, one is apt to have a much clearer and deeper impression of Quassia, if he has not only seen it, and heard its name, but has also experienced its bitter taste.

In my work on "Memory Training" I have called attention to the case of a pupil—a medical student preparing for examination—whose sense of the perception of names was weak, and who, consequently, had a poor memory for the names of things. This student, however, had a remarkably strong sense of eye-perception. I took advantage of the latter fact, and really enabled him to pass his examination with flying colors by reason of the same, whereas, otherwise, he would undoubtedly have failed. I fixed in his mind a clear perception of the names of the principal muscles of the body, the principal nerves, and the bones of the human skeleton, by having him prepare a large chart of these things, each in its proper place, with the names of each clearly marked in large letters upon it so as to positively identify it. I then taught him to make a strong, clear, positive visualization of this chart so prepared, so that he could call the whole picture, or series of pictures, before his mental vision at will. When examination-day arrived, he simply called before his mental vision the series of pictures, one at a time when needed, each bone, muscle, and nerve having its proper label affixed in the picture. The young man was practically "letter perfect" in those particular branches. I had also prepared for him a system of charts relating to other subjects, in which a system of classification was followed, and he managed to visualize these also, with excellent results. It is pleasant to be able to report that his future life showed that this system had greatly strengthened his perceptive powers and, naturally, also his memory.

Rule 10. In forming perceptive-impressions of an object or subject, endeavor to associate the same with as many pleasant "feelings" as possible, thus adding to the interesting quality of the impressions. We find it usually much easier to think of pleasant and interesting things, than the reverse.

This rule will be referred to in subsequent portions of this book. It has a direct relation to the subject considered under the head of Rule 2.

Rule 11. In analyzing and classifying an object or subject, for the purpose of obtaining clear and strong perceptive-impressions regarding it, endeavor to NAME the minor points or details whenever possible—if you do not know the correct name, at least give it some name of your own to identify it.

Names may be said to be crystallized perceptions, and the idea of the name usually brings into consciousness the ideas of the several details and characteristics of the thing expressed by the name. It is very much harder to think of things for which we have no names, than of those associated in our minds with names. Names and words are the counters with which we play the game of thinking. Without words it would be very difficult, if not indeed impossible, to think intelligently upon most subjects. As thought progresses, names are coined to crystallize the ideas. Avoid the "thingamabob," or "what-you-may-call-em" methods of thinking. Think in as clear terms as possible, and your thought currents will be likewise clear.

Note. As clear, deep, and strong Perception is one of the essential elements of an Efficient Memory, it follows that whatever will cultivate Perception will tend to improve the Memory. Therefore, the practice of the principles and rules of Efficient Perception, as given in this chapter, will inevitably result in greatly improving the Memory of the student.

The Mastery of Emotion

The average person is likely to regard the emotional phase of mental activity as merely an incidental and subordinate one. He is in the habit of thinking that men and women go through life guided by their reason and intellect, steering their bark by the compass of understanding and judgment; he is apt to think that while they experience more or less Feeling and Emotion, as their bark of life proceeds on its journey, still these play but a subordinate and comparatively unimportant part in the work of mapping out and steering the course of the ship.

But the above stated general opinion of the average man is sadly in error. Instead of being an unimportant and subordinate phase of the mental life of the individual, the psychologist knows Feeling and Emotion to be the great incentives to action, and the great motive-power of mental and physical manifestations. Even Intellect, that supposed monarch of the mental world, really is "under the thumb" of that "power behind the throne" which we know as Feeling and Emotion. Not only do we act according to our feelings, but in most cases we also think according to them. Instead of reasoning coldly and without prejudice, we really generally reason along the lines of our strong feelings.

Instead of finding real "reasons" for our actions, we usually seek merely for "excuses" to justify our actions in accordance with our feelings.

A writer has said on this point: "There are but few persons who are able to detach themselves, even in a small degree, from their feelings, so as to decide questions cold-bloodedly by pure reason or intellectual effort. Moreover, there are but few persons whose wills are guided by pure reason; their feelings supply the motive for the majority of the acts of will. The intellect, even when used, is generally employed to better carry out the dictates of Feeling and Desire. Much of our reasoning is performed in order to justify our feelings, or to find proofs for the position dictated by our desires, feelings, sympathies, prejudices, or sentiments. It has been said that 'men seek not reasons, but excuses, for their actions.' "

In the preceding chapters we have seen the important part played by Interest in the activities of the Attention; and we have seen that Attention was the ruler of Perception. This being so, it follows that Interest is largely influential in determining what perceptive-impressions we shall accept, and which we shall refuse to accept. And as these impressions are really the material from which we weave our thoughts, it follows that our thoughts and ideas are largely determined by our Interest. And, when we begin to analyze Interest, we find that it is the child of Feeling and Emotion. We like certain things, and our Interest follows our likes; then our Attention follows our Interest; and our Perception follows our Attention; and our thoughts and ideas are built up out of our Perceptions. So we find that our thoughts and ideas have been influenced, even before their birth, by Feeling and Emotion.

A writer says of this: "Feeling guards the very outer gate of knowledge, and determines largely what shall or shall not enter therein. It is one of the constantly appearing paradoxes of psychology, that while feelings have originally arisen from attention, it is equally true that attention depends largely upon the interest resulting from the feelings. This is readily admitted in the case of involuntary attention, which always goes out toward objects of interest and feeling, but it is likewise true of even voluntary attention, which we direct to something of greater or more nearly ultimate interest than the things of more immediate interest."

Another writer says: "By an act of will I may resolve to turn my attention to something—say a passage in a book. But if, after the preliminary process of adjustment of the mental eye, the object opens up no interesting phase, all the willing in the world will not produce a calm, settled state of concentration. The will introduces mind and object, but it can not force an attachment between them. No compulsion of attention ever succeeded in making a young child cordially embrace and appropriate, by an act of concentration, an unsuitable and therefore uninteresting object. "We thus see that even voluntary attention is not removed from the sway of interest. What the will does is to determine the kind of interest that shall prevail at the moment."

The memory, as is well known, will store away and recall more readily the items which prove interesting to the feelings than those which are the contrary. So true is this that it is one of the cardinal points of memory training that one should endeavor to arouse an interest in the things to be remembered; or at least to associate them with things which are interesting. Likewise, psychologists know that the imagination prefers to work with interesting materials stored away in the memory, and usually balks when required to build with materials of the opposite character. In these two fields of mental activity, Interest (and consequently Feeling) is the principal determining factor. And as our thinking is largely dependent upon these two phases of mental activity, it is seen that Feeling is all-important in deciding what we shall think of.

And, not only what we shall think of, but also how we shall think, is seen to be determined by our Feelings. As a writer says: "Our judgments are affected by our feelings. It is much easier to approve of the actions of some person whom we like, or whose views accord with our own, than of an individual whose personality and views are distasteful to us. It is very difficult to prevent prejudice, for or against anything, from influencing our judgments. It is also true that 'we find that for which we look' in things and persons, and that which we expect and look for is often dependent upon our feelings. If we dislike a person or thing we usually perceive no end of undesirable qualities in him or it; while if we are favorably inclined we easily find many admirable qualities in the same person or thing. A little change in our feeling often results in the formation of an entirely new set of judgments regarding a person or thing."

Another writer says: "On the one hand the emotions are favorable to intellectual action, since they supply the interest one feels in study. One may feel intensely concerning a certain subject, and be all the better student. Hence the emotions are not, as was formerly thought, entirely hostile to intellectual action. Emotion often quickens the perception, burns things indelibly into the memory, and doubles the rapidity of thought. On the other hand, strong feelings often vitiate every operation of the intellect.

"They cause us to see what we wish to, to remember only what interests our narrow feeling at the time, and to reason from selfish data only. Emotion puts the magnifying end of the telescope to our intellectual eyes where our own interests are concerned, the minimizing end when we are looking at the interest of others. Thought is deflected when it passes through an emotional medium, just as a sunbeam is when it strikes water."

And, finally, when we come to consider that high mental phase which we call "the will," we find that it is practically entirely dependent upon the desire mental states for its motive-power. The will operates in accordance with the strongest desire of the moment, or the average of the strongest desires of the moment; and Desire is the offspring or development of Feeling and Emotion. So that, in the end, the will is perceived to depend upon the feeling and emotional phases of mental activity for its inciting motives and for its direction.

In view of the great importance of the Feelings and Emotions in the work of our mental activities, it surely behooves the individual who wishes to develop, cultivate and unfold the Master Mind to carefully study, analyze, and consider the nature and character of Feeling and Emotion, and to seek to discover the principles, which actuate their activities. This he must do if he is desirous of mastering, controlling, and managing them. The feelings and emotions are excellent servants, and may be set to work by the Master Mind with the greatest effect. But, at the same time, if allowed to exercise unrestrained and unqualified mastery themselves, they will prove tyrants. If the Master Mind permits the Feelings and Emotions to exercise unqualified control over the mental kingdom, then it is not truly a Master Mind. The true Master Mind impresses its dominion upon the Feelings and Emotions, and then sets them to work in the right direction. In fact, it is by means of the powers of Feeling and Emotion that the Master Mind accomplishes much of its best work. This fact should be borne in mind by the reader of this book who is desirous of developing the Master Mind.

Particularly in its phase of Desire does the Master Mind make use of Feeling and Emotion. Desire may be said to be concentrated Feeling. Before we can have ambition or aspiration, there must be desire. Before we can manifest courage or energy, there must be desire. Desire for something must underlie all life-action—desire conscious or subconscious. Abstract thought is a cold bare thing, lacking vitality and warmth—desire is filled with life, throbbing, longing, wanting, craving, insisting, and ever pressing forward into action. Desire, indeed, is the motive power of all action. "We may call desire by the favorite terms of 'ambition,' 'aspiration,' 'longing for attainment,' etc., but desire is ever the basic principle of all longing, all wishing, all wanting." And this being so, let us now consider the nature of that root of desire, which we call Feeling and Emotion.

It is very hard to correctly define a "feeling." All of us know very well what is meant by the term when it is mentioned by ourselves or by others, but we experience the greatest difficulty in defining it when asked to explain just what it really is. We know what is meant by it, only because we have experienced "feelings"; if we had never experienced these we would not be able to understand what others meant when they used the term, and, likewise, we can never expect to be able to explain the same to any other person except in relation to his own experiences thereof.

Perhaps the nearest that we can come to a definition of "a feeling" is that it is a pleasant or an unpleasant mental state. A sensation may arouse a state of feeling, or it may not do so. There are many sensations that are neither pleasant nor yet unpleasant. I touch the desk before me, but the sensation of the touch thereof is neither pleasant nor unpleasant. I may touch something else, and the sensation results in an unpleasant feeling; and the touch of a third thing may awaken a pleasant feeling. As a psychologist has well said: "My feelings belong to myself; but my sensations seem to belong to the object which caused them."

Feelings may arise from either (a) one's own bodily states, or else (b) from ideas already in the mind, or called into consciousness by the sense-impressions caused by outside things by the law of association. Likewise, feelings are said to be capable of measurement according to the standards of (a) quality, or (b) quantity. In both of these measurements the basic standard of "pleasantness and unpleasantness" is involved, of course. And these standards are constantly being used by us in determining the nature of our feelings.

We often fail to recognize the vital importance of our feelings in our everyday life, thought, and actions. As the old stoic philosophers pointed out, if our sensations were robbed of the element of feeling, we would never make any choice between things or actions, for all things would seem alike to us, and all of equal value. The "feeling value" of sensations determines our attitude toward them and the things they represent in our minds. As a writer has well said: "The phenomena of the world have value for us only insofar as they affect our feelings. If a thing fails to interest us, that is, fails to touch our feelings at any point, we pass by that thing unheeded. Much of what people say to us passes in at one ear and out at the other; but if we are told of the death of a parent, the effect of the announcement may never pass away. Our feelings have been touched, and we shall never again be the same persons. A studied insult or a signal triumph affects us more powerfully than many other things, only because it appeals more deeply to feeling. Decisions in this world are generally, at last, made at the bar of feeling. It is a severer impeachment to say that a person outrages our feelings than that he is illogical."

The quality of feelings is determined principally by the fact of their respective pleasant or unpleasant effect upon us. We gauge sensations, perceptions, and ideas by this basic standard; and classify them as either pleasant, unpleasant, or neutral, in quality. A writer says: "Life is largely a struggle to secure a pleasurable quality in feeling, and to rush away from a painful attribute. Almost anyone will go to a window to look at a bright rainbow, because it gives him pleasure. We do not look straight at the sun, because we wish to avoid a painful feeling. Many of us dislike to see ulcers or deformity for the same reason."

The same sensation or perception may awaken different qualities of Feeling in us under different circumstances. For instance, as a writer has said: "You drop your purse, and you see it lying on the ground as you stoop to pick it up, with no feeling of pleasure or pain; but if you see it after you have lost it and have hunted for it for a long time in vain, you have a pronounced feeling of pleasure." And, again, one may find pleasure in the taste of a certain food at one time, but after having eaten a large quantity of the food you may lose the pleasant feeling and experience merely a neutral feeling toward it; and, finally, if you have over-eaten of the food, and have been made nauseated by it, you may for some time afterward experience an unpleasant feeling toward it—the very thought of it may make you feel uncomfortable.

Then, again, there is a great difference in the

quantity or intensity value of the same class of feelings. A writer illustrates this as follows: "The discomfort from the bite of a mosquito is not so massive as the pain from a large bruise or a broken limb. Any boy would say that a heaping teaspoonful of ice-cream would give him more pleasure than an amount the size of a pea." In the same way, some ideas, recollections, or results of the imagination, will be found far more intensively pleasant than others in the same class; and the same is, of course, true regarding the unpleasant mental states of this kind. In either of these instances we will find that we will move in the direction of the feeling giving us the greater degree or quantity of pleasant feeling, and that we will move away from the feeling giving us the greater degree or quantity of unpleasant feeling. In fact, practically all of our changes and choices follow this rule.

A writer has said: "All forms of pleasure and pain are called feelings. Between the pleasure which comes from eating a peach, and that which results from solving a difficult problem, or learning good news of a friend, or thought of the progress of civilization—between the pain that results from a cut in the hand, and that which results from the failure of a long cherished plan, or the death of a friend—there

174

is a long distance. But the one group are all pleasures; the other all pains. And, whatever the source of the pleasure or the pain, it is alike feeling." Another writer has said: "The feelings depending upon bodily states arise either from inherited tendencies and inclinations, or from acquired habits and experience. A physical activity that has become the habit of the race, and which has been conducive to the welfare of the race in the past, tends toward pleasurable feeling in the individual; as for instance, hunting, fishing, traveling, swimming, etc., as well as the fundamental wants of the physical organism, such as eating, drinking, rest, sleep, etc. Many of our tendencies and feelings are inherited in this way. The feelings depending upon ideas which may also arise from inheritance, and many of our mental tendencies and ideas have come down to us from the past in this way."

"Other feelings arising from ideas and memories depend upon our individual past experience, influenced largely by association, suggestion, and similar causes. The ideals of those around us have a decided influence upon our feelings concerning certain things concerned therewith; the force of suggestion along these lines are very marked. Not only do we experience feelings in response to present sensations, but the recollection of some previous experience may also arouse feeling. In fact, feelings of this kind are closely bound up with memory and imagination. Persons of a vivid imagination are apt to feel more keenly than do others; they suffer more and enjoy more. Our sympathies, which depend largely upon our imaginative power, are the cause of many of our feelings of this kind.

Some psychologists make many elaborate distinctions between Feeling and Emotion; but many of those distinctions may be practically disregarded. The reader may be assisted in forming a correct idea of the true distinction by reference to the distinction between Sensation and Perception. Just as Sensation is a simple mental state which may evolve into a more complex mental state called Perception (particularly in the phase of Apperception), so is Feeling a simple mental state which may evolve into n. more complex mental state called Emotion. And just as Apperception necessitates the presence of representative ideas (i.e., the ideas arising in memory or imagination), so does Emotion require the presence thereof. Moreover, Feeling may arise from either a bodily state or an idea, while Emotion, as a rule, is dependent upon an idea for its full expression and particularly for its direction and continuance.

The following quotation from an eminent psychologist will perhaps give a clearer idea of the relation of Emotion to Feeling: "Feeling is a simple, primitive, mental state. Emotion is a more complex mental state, and it demands the presence of a representative idea to guide and prolong it. Feeling is present in all emotional states. It is a thread on which all other states are strung like beads. When representative ideas appear, the Feeling in combination with them produces Emotion. After the waters of the Missouri combine with another stream, they receive a different name, although they flow on toward the Gulf in as great body as before. Suppose we liken the Feelings due to sensation to the Missouri River; the train of representative ideas to the Mississippi before its junction with the Missouri; and Emotion to the Mississippi after the junction—after Feeling has combined with representative idea. The Emotional stream will now be broader and deeper than before. The student must beware of thinking that we have done with Feeling when we consider Emotion. Just as the waters of the Missouri flow on until they reach the Gulf, so does Feeling run through every Emotional state."

Emotion tends toward expression in physical action. Thus we frown, or smile, clench the fist, or extend the hand—or find expression of the Emotion in more complex physical actions. And, likewise it is true that the manifestation of these physical forms of expression tends to fan the fire of the Emotion. In fact, the best psychologists hold that the full force of the Emotion does not manifest itself unless the person also manifests the physical expression. And, likewise not only is the flame of the Emotion fanned and strengthened by the physical expression, but it is also prolonged and continued by the continuance of the physical expression. Consequently, a repression of the physical expression tends to deaden repress, and inhibit the full expression and manifestation of an Emotion.

Feeling and Emotion reach their highest point in the mental state which we call Desire. Feeling and Emotion are essentially inner states, while in Desire we find a state of tension in which the inner state seeks to transform itself into an outer action. Feeling and Emotion may be compared to the condition of steam in an engine before the pressure is sufficient to generate the power necessary to move the engine; when the pressure becomes sufficiently strong, the steam begins to "want" to find expression in action, and accordingly strives to force itself into the mechanism of action. Whoever has felt the pressure of a strong Desire—and who has not?—will appreciate the fitness of this illustration.

Desire is the great motive power of life. It is the great incentive to action. A man is largely what the quality and degree of his desires have led him to be. Desire is the fire which produces the steam of action. No matter how well equipped intellectually a man may be—no matter how great may be his powers of perception, reason, judgment, and discrimination—it is true that unless he also possesses a strong desire for accomplishment, the other faculties will never be brought into action. Desire is the great inciter of mental and physical activities—the arouser of the will.

Not only is our life largely determined by the nature and quality of our desires, but our accomplishments and attainments depend very materially upon the degree of our desires. The quality of desire determines in what mental path we shall travel, but the degree determines how far we shall travel. The majority of persons manifest but little desire—they want many things, it is true, but they do not want them "hard enough." Their desires end in mere wishing, and wanting—they do not reach the stage of action. Desire unexpressed is like steam in a boiler that has not reached the full intensity required to drive the engine. Increase the intensity and degree, and the steam rushes out, and in a moment the pistons are moving and the wheels revolving.

The great men in all walks of life have possessed strong desires for attainment, accomplishment, possession—the principle being the same in all these cases. Their desire was of such a degree that it reached the explosive point, and manifested in action. It is generally taught that Will is the great motive power of the mind. But this is not correct unless it is also stated that Will is but the active phase of desire. Desire is the motive power that imparts the energy to the action. The will is more like a guiding, directing force which applies the energy of the desire. Will is cold, and steely—desire is glowing with heat. The will may, and does, guide, direct, restrict, hold back, and even destroy the desire in some cases—but, nevertheless, desire supplies the energy for action.

No matter how strong a will the individual may have, unless he has a strong desire to use the will he will not use it. No matter how clearly a man may see how a thing may be done, no matter how well his reason and judgment may point out the way, no matter how clear an imagination he may possess to picture the plan of the action— unless he be possessed of the desire to act, and that in a goodly degree, then there will be no action. The individual who allows his desires to master him is to be pitied—he, alas! is not a Master Mind. But this is true of the great majority of the race, who are swayed this way and that way by their desires, and who have not as yet acquired the art of submitting their desires to the judgment of their reason and the control of their will. The man who has acquired the art of controlling and directing his desires has traveled far on the road to attainment. For, to such a man, desire becomes a faithful and efficient servant, inspiring action and interest, and therefore all the other mental faculties.

Desire, of course, is the evolved stage of Feeling and Emotion. It is the link between Emotion on one side, and Will on the other side. On its inner side, desire is but the product of various states and combinations of states of feeling and emotion; and on its outer side it merges and blends into the activities of the will. As a writer has said:

"All feeling tends to excite desire. In one aspect, desire is feeling; in another, desire is will, or an active tension which passes imperceptibly into will. How shall we distinguish between feeling and will? There is no more precise line of demarcation than exists between the Atlantic Ocean and Davis Strait. The difficulty of separating feeling from will is especially great, because there so often seems to be no break between the two processes. Whenever there is in emotion a motor element which tends to go out in action, that element is will. In some emotions, the voluntary element may be so small as to baffle detection, but the germs is there. At the threshold of each higher act of will stands desire. This is a complex mental state, and it contains the elements of both emotion and will. In every state of desire is (1) conscious feeling, and (2) conscious tension which easily passes into action."

There have been many attempts to define Desire. Perhaps the best, and clearest in its analysis of the essential qualities of Desire is that of Halleck, the psychologist, who has furnished psychology with the following definition: "Desire has for its object something that will bring pleasure or get rid of pain, immediate or remote, for the individual or for someone else in whom he is interested. Aversion, or a striving away from something, is merely the negative aspect of desire."

Halleck also explains his definition, as follows: "Desire is not always proportional to the idea of one's own selfish pleasure. Many persons, after forming an idea of the vast amount of earthly distress, desire to relieve it; and the desire goes out in action, as the benevolent societies in every city testify. Here, the individual pleasure is not the less real, but is secondary, coming from the pleasure of others. The idea of the near often raises a stronger desire than the remote. A child frequently prefers a thing immediately, if it is only one-tenth as good as something he might have a year hence. A student often desires more the leisure of today than the success of future years. Though admonished to study, he wastes his time and thus loses incomparably greater future pleasure when he is tossed to the rear in the struggle for existence."

Many persons, particularly those of untrained will and uncultivated intellect, are moved to action upon the desires along the lines of pure impulse. A psychologist says of impulsive actions: "The psychological condition of impulse is, that with the momentary feeling and sensation should be combined a more or less clear idea of something which may augment the pleasure or diminish the pain of the moment." Persons who have trained the will, and cultivated the intellect, however, are not so apt to be moved into action upon the momentary impulse. On the contrary, those persons bring the intellect into play, and bring before the Ego other ideas concerning the value and effect of the proposed action. They balance one set of ideas against another; they deliberate over the matter, and weigh the advantages against the disadvantages of the proposed action. Here, of course, is performed the act of comparing several sorts of feelings, emotions, and desires, to the end that the most desirable one presenting itself is chosen.

A writer has well illustrated a conflict of desires in the story of Jeppe, a character in a well-known French comedy. Jeppe, who is very fond of tippling, wants a drink very much. His wife gives him money with which to buy a cake of soap. He knows from experience that if he wastes this money in drink, he will be soundly beaten by his wife. He wants the drink, but he wants to escape the beating—and then begins the fight of desires in his mind. Jeppe says to himself: "My stomach says drink, my back says soap." Jeppe has a hard time trying to decide which desire is strongest. He compares the idea of the pleasure, with that of the pain, and tries to find out which is the strongest in his desire-world. Finally he asks himself: "Is not my stomach more to me than my back?" Then he answers himself: "I say yes!" And he buys the drink, though knowing that he will get a beating from his wife when she catches him. But, as a writer has well said: "Jeppe's decision to drink might not have been carried into action, had he seen his wife waiting for him with a club at the tavern door."

As we have seen, human beings are moved to action by their Feelings, Emotions, and Desires—and that the essence of the said mental states may be summed up in the statement that: Men act from motives of securing that which will bring them the greatest amount of pleasure, or the least amount of pain, immediate or remote, for themselves or for others in whom they are interested. In short, men ever strive for Pleasure, which means: "that which pleases, gratifies, satisfies, comforts, or makes happy, joyous, or glad"; and away from Pain, which means: "that which displeases, fails to gratify, produces discomfort and dissatisfaction, or makes one unhappy, sorrowful, or sad." Pleasure is always a profit to the individual; and Pain always a loss: at least in the ordinary estimation that men place upon emotional-values

The Categories of Feeling

We have seen that Desire is the great motive power which leads to thought and action. "We have also seen that Desire is the evolved state of Feeling and Desire. Therefore, before we can intelligently understand how to manage and control, direct and give force to our Desires, we must first understand something about the shape, form, and pluses which Feeling and Emotion take upon themselves in our mental world. Most of us have very vague ideas about the many phases of Feeling, under which it manifests itself to us. We are apt to think that Feeling and Emotion is confined to a comparatively small class of strong emotions and passions, and we ignore the many other forms of manifestation which it assumes.

Any consciousness of "like" or "dislike" is a state of some kind or phase of Feeling. We "like" or "dislike" things simply because we are experiencing a feeling concerning them. If we had no Feeling concerning a thing we would not want or desire any one kind of things in preference to another kind—all things would seem alike to us, and we would not want to have or experience anything whatsoever, nor would we fear to experience anything whatsoever. This would be almost equivalent to being dead, for Life is composed largely of feelings, wants, desires, cravings, longings, fears, likes and dislikes, and the actions arising therefrom.

We shall now present for your inspection the following list of the several classes or categories of Feeling and Emotion, all of which, of course, are constantly striving to express themselves in action by means of the pressure and power of Desire. Here follows the said list:

1. Elemental Feelings.

2. The Affections.

Return to top

3. Social Feelings.

4. Moral Feelings.

5. Religious Feelings.

Return to top

6. Esthetic Feelings.

7. Intellectual Feelings.

The feelings and emotions in each and every one of the above categories are found to manifest in two directions, positive and negative phases, as follows: (1) Positive Phase of DESIRE for the objects of the feeling; and (2) Negative Phase of FEAR, that the individual may not attain, or may lose, these objects. We now present to your consideration each of the above classes of Feeling and Emotion, in further detail.

1. The Elemental Feelings. In this category are found the feelings and emotions which are basic and elemental in the human race, and which have to do with the preservation of the life of the individual man, his physical welfare and general material comfort. In this class of feelings there is little or no feeling concerning the welfare or happiness of others, as such, the feeling manifested being characteristically egotistic or "selfish." In this class we find the feelings concerned with the satisfaction of hunger and thirst, the securing of comfortable clothing, the securing and holding of comfortable living quarters or place of abode, the elemental sexual impulses, the lust for physical power and superiority, and the spirit of combat and strife arising from the original search for, and the subsequent securing and retention of the objects above noted.

This class of feelings may be said to be practically instinctive, or as having reached the individual through heredity and race-memory. Instincts are held to be the result of the past experiences of the race, transmitted by heredity, and preserved in the basic memory of the race. Their end is of course the preservation of the species, through the preservation and survival of the individual, and through his production of offspring. The real end and aim of the instinctive feeling is seldom perceived by the individual manifesting it, for the same lies deep below the surface in the emotional being of the man. So far as is concerned the individual experiencing the feeling and expressing it in action, these feelings have to do only with his momentary satisfaction, pleasure, and comfort; he has no thought of race-preservation in his mind—but Nature has a deeper meaning than the individual perceives.

In this class of feelings we find the so-called "elemental passions," which, however, are merely strong manifestations of the feelings which have just been described, and which bring in their train the feelings of hate, revenge, jealousy, desire for material possessions and wealth; as well as strong desires for the objects and things which will tend to secure for the individual the things forming the object of his basic desires, or which will tend to enable him to retain, or add to such things.

In this class of feelings we also find those concerned with the personal pride of vanity of the individual, and which has to do with his self-regard. Even the most elemental savage manifests a high degree of vanity, and is filled with a certain kind of pride. In fact, even some of the lower animals manifest emotions of this kind. Some psychologists have traced this emotion back to the desire of this elemental man to excite desire in others, but the feeling is probably more complex than this. This emotion causes men and women to indulge in many actions otherwise unexplainable, and includes within its limits the desire for personal adornment and finery—the latter being regarded by some writers as having arisen from a desire to attract mates. But whatever may have been the roots of this class of feelings, they undoubtedly add materially to the self-satisfaction of the individual, and play an important part in his life.

2. The Affections. The feelings within the present category may be regarded as having evolved from those in the preceding category, during the process of the evolution of the race. From the elemental passion of mating has evolved the much higher forms of affection for the

190

mate, and the desire for his or her welfare and comfort. Likewise, from the elemental sense of ownership, and the protection thereof, which included the offspring, there has evolved the higher phases of love of and devotion to one's children, extending in many cases to the making of great sacrifices for their welfare.

A writer says of this class of affections, and the evolution thereof from more elementary feelings: "From instinctive sexual love and the racial instinct have developed the higher affection of man for woman, and woman for man, in all their beautiful manifestations; and, likewise, the love of the parent for the child. The first manifestation of altruistic feeling was expressed in the love of the creature for its mate, and in the love of the parents for their offspring. In certain forms of life where the association of the sexes is merely for the moment, and is not followed by protection, mutual aid, and companionship, there is found an absence of mutual affection of any kind, the only feeling being an elemental reproductive instinct bringing the male and female together for the moment—an almost reflex activity.

In the same way, in the case of certain animals (the rattlesnake, for instance) in which the young are able to protect themselves from birth, there is seen a total absence of parental affection or the return hereof. Human love between the sexes, in its higher and lower degrees, is a natural evolution from passional emotion of an elemental order, the evolution being due to the development of social, ethical, moral, and aesthetic emotion arising from the necessities of the increasing complexity and development of human life.

As man advanced in the scale his affectional feelings enlarged their inclusive circle. The circle took in not only the mate and offspring, but also the nearer relations; and to a lesser degree, certain members of the same tribe—"friends" began to be recognized, and the affectional feeling of friendship began to manifest itself in the race. As the race has evolved, the individual has tended toward feeling and manifesting a larger and fuller degree and extent of this class of affectional feeling. Many individuals will make great sacrifices for relations and friends, and in numerous instances the individual may go so far in this direction as to ruin himself by mistaken and ill-advised kindness in this direction.

3. Social Feelings. The feelings within the present category are also the outgrowth of the elemental feelings. Early in the history of the race (and in fact in the forms of life antedating

the human race) it was found that it was mutually advantageous for a number of individuals to form in groups for self-protection, and increased efficiency in hunting, and obtaining food. The animals recognize this by their habit of herding, or forming themselves into flocks. And men began to associate in tribes, and later in nations. Man began to be "a social animal" early in his history. And from the more simple feelings associated with this grouping has grown the more complex and higher social feelings of the advanced members of the race today.

In the category of the Social Feelings are found those feelings which are concerned with the general welfare of the community, and of the state; which lead to the performance of what are felt to be duties and obligations rightfully due toward society and our fellow-men. In this category are found "sociability," love of companionship, tenderness toward association; and also civic virtue, law-abiding actions, charity, mutual aid, the alleviation of poverty and suffering of others, the erection of asylums, orphanages, and homes for the aged, hospitals for the sick, and association for general charitable work. The many forms of patriotism and devotion to one's country are also found in this class, although there are other emotional factors present in such cases.

4. Moral Feelings. The feelings within this category also have evolved from the elementary feelings of the race. They are closely bound up with the Social Feelings, and may be regarded as the evolution thereof, or as a phase thereof. This class of feelings arise from a feeling that one "ought to" observe certain formal codes of conduct, or general laws, laid down by some superior authority, or else tacitly adopted as proper by the general society of which the individual happens to be a member.

In many these feelings are closely associated with the Religious Feelings, but there is a distinction to be noted here. We may find persons of a very high degree of moral conduct, and ethical tendencies, who may be lacking in the religious emotions. And, too often, we find persons who profess, and seemingly experience, marked degrees of religious emotion and feeling, but who fall short of adhering to many of the precepts of the higher morality of their times and country. But, it is of course true that the highest religious teachings seek to encourage high ethical and moral emotions and actions.

A writer makes the following important distinction: "We must here make the distinction between those manifesting the actions termed

194

ethical and moral because they feel that way, on the one hand, and on the other hand those who merely comply with the conventional requirements of custom and the law because they fear the consequences of the violation thereof. The first class have the true social, ethical, and moral feelings, tastes, ideals, and inclinations; while the second manifest merely the elementary feelings of self-preservation and selfish prudence. The first class are 'good' because they feel that way and find it natural to be so; while the second class are 'good' merely because they have to be so, or else be punished by legal penalty or public opinion, loss of prestige, loss of financial support, etc."

The same writer interestingly states: "Theology explains the moral feelings as resulting from conscience, which it holds to be a special faculty of the mind, or soul, divinely given. Science, while admitting the existence of the state of feeling which we call 'conscience,' at the same time ignores its claimed supernatural origin, and ascribes it to the effects of evolution, heredity, experience, education, suggestion, and general environment. Conscience, according to this last view, is a compound of intellectual and emotional states. Conscience, therefore, in this view is not an infallible guide, but depends entirely upon the hereditary and environmental history of the individual; and accompanies the moral and ethical codes and customs of the race at any particular stage of its history.

5. Religious Feelings. This class of feelings play a very important part in the everyday life of the individuals composing the race. There are but few persons who are not more or less influenced in their actions by their religious feelings. Religious Feelings may be defined as: "The feelings resulting from a belief in a Divine Supreme Being, and an emotion of love for and devotion to this Being, and a desire to adore and worship the same." Darwin says that the feeling of Religious Devotion is a highly complex one, consisting of love, complete submission to an exalted and mysterious superior, a strong sense of dependence, fear, reverence, gratitude, hope for the future, and perhaps other elements. Herbert Spencer, while holding that man originally obtained his idea of religion from the savage's primeval world of dreams, ghosts, etc., nevertheless held that, "The ultimate form of religious consciousness is the final development of a consciousness which at the outset contained a germ of thought obscured by multitudinous errors."

But whatever one may think concerning the origin of Religious Feeling, few will dispute the fact that the essence thereof is an inner experience rather than an intellectual conception. The emotional element is never lacking in the full religious experience and manifestation. A purely intellectual religion is naught but a philosophy; religion without feeling and emotion is an anomaly, and would be little more than a "school of ethical culture." As a writer has said: "In all true religion there exists a feeling of inner assurance and faith, love, awe, dependence, submission, reverence, gratitude, hope—and often fear as well."

5. Aesthetic Feelings. In this category of feelings are included the various feelings concerned with Beauty or Taste. Beauty is: "That quality of assemblage of qualities in an object which gives the eye or ear intense pleasure." Taste (as used in this connection) is: "The faculty of discerning beauty, order, congruity, proportion, symmetry, or whatever constitutes excellence, particularly in the fine arts and literature."

A writer says: "The possession of taste insures grace and beauty in the works of an artist, and the avoidance of all that is low and mean. It is as often the result of an inmate sense of beauty as of art education, and no genius can compensate for the want of it. Tastes differ so much among individuals, nations, or in different ages and conditions of civilization that it is utterly impossible to set up a standard of taste applicable to all men and to all stages of society."

The roots of the aesthetic feelings probably are to be found in attempts at personal decoration on the part of savages—these, in turn, probably having originated in the feeling of vanity, or the desire to attract the other sex. However, even among some of the lower animals we find evidences of elementary feelings of this class, as evidenced by the selection of mates on account of attractive coloring, or attractive form; and also by the habits of certain birds which adorn their nests with bits of colored material, shells, etc. Herbert Spencer says that the aesthetic feelings are separated from the functions vitally requisite to sustain life, and that not until the latter are at least reasonably well satisfied do the former begin to manifest themselves in evidence.

The pleasure derived from the sight or hearing of beautiful things seems to be a phase of sensory excitement, though it is difficult to classify the same. We know that we do experience pleasant sensations from the perceptions of that which we consider to possess beauty, but we do not know "just why" certain things possess the power to so move us to fueling. Association

and habit undoubtedly have much to do with
determining our standards of beauty, for there
is the widest differences manifest in the tastes
of different individuals, and different races,
and different classes of people. There seems to
be no universal standard of beauty; and what
one set of persons may consider very beautiful, another set may regard as hideously ugly.
Moreover, the same set of persons may consider
a certain kind of things beautiful for a time,
and afterward regard the same kind of things as
lacking in beauty—we have an example of this
in the changing fashions in clothing, art, music,
literature, etc.

A writer says: "There are fashions in art and
music, as in clothes; and what is thought beautiful today may be deemed hideous tomorrow.
This is not due to the evolution of taste, for in
many cases the old fashions are revived, and
are again considered beautiful. There is, moreover, the effect of the association of the object
of emotion with certain events or persons. The
association renders the thing popular, and therefore agreeable and beautiful for the time being.
The suggestion in a story will often cause the
beauty of a certain scene, or the harmony of a
certain piece of music, to dawn upon thousands
of persons. Some noted person sets the seal
of approval upon a certain picture or musical

composition, and lo! the multitude calls it beautiful. It must not be supposed, however, that the crowd always counterfeits this sense of beauty and excellence which has been suggested to it; on the contrary, genuine aesthetic feeling often results from the discovery so made."

A writer says: "The vulgar are pleased with great masses of color, especially red, orange, and purple, which give their coarse, nervous organization the requisite stimulus. The refined, with nerves of less caliber, but greater discriminativeness, require delicate combinations of complementaries, and prefer neutral tints to the glare of the primary hues. Children and savages love to dress in all the hues of the rainbow."
In the same way we find some persons taking great delight in cheap popular songs, considered "trashy" and very unpleasant by others; likewise, some revel in "rag-time" music, while others find the same almost unbearable. A writer says of this: "It is said that aesthetics cannot be treated in a scientific way because there is no standard of taste.

'De gustibus nori est disputandurn' ('there is no disputing about tastes') is an old proverb. Of two equally intelligent persons, the one may like a certain book, the other dislike it. While it is true that the standard of taste is a varying one within certain limits, it is no more so than that of morals. As men's nervous systems, education, and associations differ, we may scientifically conclude that their tastes must differ. The greater the uniformity in the factors, the less does the product vary. On the other hand, within certain limits, the standard of aesthetics is relatively uniform. It is fixed by the majority of intelligent people of any age and country. To estimate the standard by which to judge of the correctness of language or of the literary taste of any era, we examine the conversations of the best speakers, the works of the standard writers.

Another writer says: "It is claimed by some of the best authorities that to develop the finer and higher aesthetic feelings and emotions, we must learn to find beauty and excellence in things removed from ourselves or our selfish interests. The narrow, selfish emotions kill the aesthetic feelings—the two cannot exist together. The person whose thoughts are centered on himself or herself very rarely finds beauty or excellence in works of art or music." Another writer says: "Good taste is the progressive product of progressing fineness and discrimination in the nerves, educated attention, high and noble emotional construction, and increasing intellectual faculties."

But, whatever may be the real explanation of the nature and origin of this great class of feelings, the best authorities agree in the statement that they exert a great influence over the thoughts and actions of men and women—even where the individuals may not claim to possess any particular aesthetic tastes. One has but to stop and think a moment of how many times he says (or thinks) "I like the looks of that one," and "I don't like the looks of that thing"; or "that sounds good to me," or the reverse; in order to perceive how strongly his tastes are in evidence and action. From the uncultured barbarian to the most highly cultured individual of our civilization, there is always to be found a "like" and a "dislike" concerning the looks and sounds of things. Vary as greatly as do the favorite standards of taste of different peoples, and different individuals, yet each is strongly influenced by that standard, and his actions are in accordance therewith.

7. Intellectual Feelings. In this category of feelings we find those phases of emotion or feeling which arise from the exercise of the intellectual faculties, or the contemplation of the results of a similar exercise on the part of others. The faculties which are most concerned in the production and manifestation of this class of feelings are those of perception, memory, imagina-

tion, reason, judgment, and the logical faculties in general. Those who have acquired the art of voluntary attention to a high degree, and who manifest the same in the work of the constructive imagination or creative mental activity, usually experience this class of feeling quite strongly.

A writer says of this: "The exercise of perception, if we are skilled therein, gives us a pleasurable feeling, and if we succeed in making an interesting or important discovery by reason thereof, we experience a strong degree of emotional satisfaction. Likewise, we experience agreeable feelings when we are able to remember distinctly something which might well have been forgotten, or when we succeeded in recalling something which bad escaped our memory for the moment. In the same way, the exercise of the imagination is a source of great pleasure in many cases, in the direction of writing, planning, inventing, and other creative processes, or even in the building of air castles. The exercise of the logical faculties gives great pleasure to those in whom these faculties are well developed."

Another writer says: "There was probably not a happier moment in Newton's life than when he had succeeded in demonstrating that the same power which caused the apple to fall held the moon and the planets in their orbits. When Watts discovered that steam might be harnessed like a horse, when an inventor succeeds in perfecting a labor-lightening device, "whenever an obscurity is cleared away, the reason for a thing understood, and a baffling instance brought under a general law, intellectual emotion exists." We feel assured that the student of this book who will put into active practice the principles and exercises given therein concerning the Master Mind will find a high degree of pleasure in the task and attainment, and will thus have in his own experience a typical illustration of the nature and power of the intellectual emotions and feelings.

This class of feelings, of course, is the result of the long evolution of the mind of the race. The savage scarcely knows these feelings, and the uncultured person experiences them to only a slight degree. It is only when men cultivate and employ voluntary attention in the direction of "study," investigation, and logical thought, that they find these feelings strongly in evidence. The student of philosophy or science has at his command a world of pleasurable feelings which are comparatively unknown to the great masses of persons.

General Conclusions. The student who has carefully read what has been said regarding the Feelings and Emotions, will have perceived the great motive power possessed by these mental states. He will have seen how the life of the individual is largely influenced by the presence and power of Feeling and Emotion, both in the direction of thought and that of action. This being perceived, the thoughtful student will also see the desirability of the individual carefully cultivating his emotional nature, so that he may strengthen those classes of feelings which are conducive to his welfare and success, and to inhibit or repress those which are harmful and destructive in their effects. He will, indeed, see that such cultivation and control is absolutely essential to the one who wishes to develop into a Master Mind, and a Mind Master. The Mastery of Mind has as one of its essential principles the mastery of the emotional nature, and its employment in the direction of influencing and stimulating thought and action.

In the succeeding chapter, the most approved methods of cultivating and controlling the emotional phases of the mind will be presented for your careful consideration and instruction. We trust that you will fully appreciate the importance of the same, for much depends upon your mastery of these phases of your mental nature if you desire to become a Master Mind.

The Mastery of Desire

The Mastery of Desire does not mean (as some suppose) the "killing out" of all Desire. In fact, as all careful students of the subject well know, it would be impossible to kill out all Desire, for the very act of "killing out" would be actually, itself, a response to a desire—a desire not to desire, as it were. Mastery of Desire really means the control, management, and direction of Desire by the Ego. The Ego may decide that a certain set of desires be repressed, or shut off, and prevented from expression in action or thought. Again, it may decide that certain desires be encouraged, cultivated, and stimulated, so that they may be able to exert a greater pressure and power in expression in thought and action. And, finally, it may decide to direct into a certain channel the force of a certain desire, so that some particular action may receive its concentrated and firmly directed power. In all of these cases, the Ego manifests Mastery of Desire.

In beginning the study of the Mastery of Desire, however, we must, of course, begin with the subject of the handling, direction, culture and control of the Feelings and Emotions, for these are the "stuff" of which Desire is made. The Ego must learn how to manufacture certain grades and kinds of Feeling and Emotion into Desire, and at the same time to discard and throw into the "scrap pile" other kinds of Feelings and Emotions which would make only the wrong kind of Desire.

How to Restrain Feelings, Emotions, or Desires

The general rules for the restraint of any class of feelings, emotions, and the desires arising therefrom, are as follows:

1. Refrain as far as possible from the physical expression of the feeling, or emotion, or the desire arising therefrom, which are deemed objectionable.

2. Refuse to permit the formation of the habit of expressing in action the feeling, or emotion, or the desire arising therefrom, which are deemed objectionable.

3. Refuse to dwell upon the idea or mental picture of the object or subject exciting the feeling, or emotion, or the desire arising therefrom, which are deemed objectionable.

4. Cultivate the class of feelings or emotions, or the desires arising therefrom, which are opposed to those deemed objectionable.

Let us now consider each one of these rules in further detail.

1. Refrain from the Physical Expression. A strong feeling or emotion, and the desire arising therefrom, tends toward expression in physical action of some kind. In fact, the feeling is said not to have been fully manifested unless this outward expression is had in at least some degree. This being so, it is seen that if one refrains from the physical expression he has done something to prevent the full manifestation of the feeling.

So closely are the two—feelings and their physical expression—connected, that some psychologists have, actually held that the physical expression precedes and practically causes the mental state of feeling. This, however, is not the commonly accepted view, the latter being that the mental state precedes and causes the physical expression. One has but to experience the feeling of anger to know that the same is accompanied by a faster beating of the heart, a tight pressing-together of the lips, a frowning brow, narrowed eyes, and clenched fists, and a raised voice. Likewise, one who has experienced the emotion of fear knows how his jaw dropped, his legs trembled, his eye opened widely, etc. But few realize that if the man who begins to feel the rise of the feeling of anger will but positively refuse to press his lips together, to frown, to narrow his eyes, to clench his fists—and, above all, to raise his voice—he will find that the feeling of anger will cease to increase, and that in fact it will gradually die away and disappear.

Some men in important positions make it an invariable rule to maintain an even, low tone of voice when they are threatened with a rush of angry feeling—they have found that such a plan prevents them from "flying into a rage," and enables them to "keep their temper," even under the most trying circumstances. And, in passing, it may be said that such a course will often result in the other person to the quarrel also lowering his voice, and abating his angry feeling.

A writer says: "There is a mutual action and reaction between emotional mental states and the physical expression thereof; each in a measure being the cause of the other, and each at the same time being the effect of the other. For instance: in the case of anger, the object causing the feeling tends to produce, almost simultaneously, the emotional state of anger and the several physical manifestations which usually accompany that state. There then occurs a series of mental and physical reactions. The mental state acts upon the physical expression and intensifies it. The physical expression in turn reacts upon the mental state, and induces a more intense degree of emotional feeling. And so on, each acting and reacting upon the other, until mental state and physical expression reach their highest point and then begin to subside from exhaustion of energy. It is an established fact of psychology that each physical expression of an emotion serves to intensify the latter—it is like pouring oil upon the fire. Likewise, it is equally true that the repression of the physical expression of an emotion tends to restrain and inhibit the emotion itself."

Another writer says: "If we watch a person growing angry, we shall see the emotion increase as he talks loud, frowns deeply, clinches his fist, and gesticulates wildly. Each expression of his passion is reflected back upon the original anger and adds fuel to the fire. If he resolutely inhibits the muscular expressions of his anger, it will not attain great intensity, and it will soon die a quiet death. Not without reason are those persons called cold-blooded who habitually restrain as far as possible the expression of their emotion; who never frown or throw any feeling into their tones, even when a wrong inflicted upon someone demands aggressive measures. There is here no wave of bodily expression to flow back and augment the emotional state."

The last quoted writer also says: "Actors have frequently testified to the fact that emotion will arise if they go through the appropriate muscular movements. In talking to actors on the stage, if they clinch the fists and frown, they often find themselves becoming really angry; if they start with counterfeit laughter, they find themselves growing cheerful. A German professor says that he cannot watch a schoolgirl's mincing step and air without feeling frivolous." Another writer, a famous psychologist, said: "Refuse to express a passion, and it dies. Count ten before venting your anger, and its occasion seems ridiculous. Whistling to keep up courage is no mere figure of speech. On the other hand, sit all day in a moping posture, sigh and reply to everything with a dismal voice, and your melancholy lingers. There is no more valuable precept in moral education than this, as all who have experience know: If we wish to conquer undesirable emotional tendencies in ourselves, we must assiduously, and in the first instance cold-bloodedly, go through the outward movements of those contrary dispositions which we wish to cultivate. Soothe the brow, brighten the eye, contract the dorsal rather than the ventral aspect of the frame, and speak in a major key, and your heart must be frigid indeed if it does not gradually thaw."

The essence, then, of the above is: Refrain so far as is possible from indulging in the physical expression of a feeling, emotion, or desire which you wish to conquer, control, and repress.

2. Refuse to Form the Habit of Expression in Action. Habits build a mental path over which the Will thereafter travels. Or, to use another figure of speech, Habit cuts a channel, through which the Will afterward flows. When you express a feeling, emotion, or desire in action you begin to form a habit; when you express it the second time the habit takes on force; and so on, each repetition widening the mental path, or deepening the mental channel over which it is easy for subsequent action to travel. The oftener the feeling, emotion, or desire travels this path of action, the stronger does it become. Habit is like the lion-cub, which while perfectly harmless when a cub, eventually grows so strong as to destroy its former master.

Refuse to give the disadvantageous feeling the exercise which it requires to promote its growth—for feelings grow and gain strength by exercise. Instead, starve it to death by refusing it the food of expression, and in time it will droop and die. Habit is a fine servant, but a poor master.

The essence, then, of the above is: Don't get into the habit of expressing in action a feeling, emotion, or desire which you wish to conquer, control, and repress.

3. Refuse to Dwell upon the Idea or Mental Picture. This rule is based upon the accepted fact of psychology that Feeling, Emotion, and Desire are fed, nourished, and strengthened by the representative idea, or mental image of the object or subject which has originally inspired them, or which is associated with that object or subject. Feelings are often caused by an idea, resulting from the process of thought or recalled in memory. Likewise they are deepened and strengthened by the recalling into consciousness of such ideas. In the same way, they are fed and nourished by ideas connected with the original object or subject by the ties of association.

A writer has said: "Feelings may be caused by an idea. The remembrance of an insult, of an act of unkindness, of a wrong done, may cause acute feeling. The memory of his dead mother's face caused the stolid Nero pain. There may be no immediately preceding change in the sense organ when an idea flashes into the mind, but the feeling may be just as pronounced as if it were. Shakespeare classified the feelings as (a) the sensuous, and (b) the ideal, when he represented the pain inflicted by the wintry wind as less severe than the memory of man's ingratitude. The ideal feelings, however, rest indirectly upon sensory foundations. A representative idea is a revived sensation, or a complex of revived sensations. Some ideas cause a joyful, others a sorrowful mental state; accordingly feelings differ qualitatively according to the idea. Our feelings also differ quantitatively according as the idea has a more or less pleasurable or painful element"

The same writer says: "The idea of a glass of water when one is not thirsty will have little effect. The mental image of a glass of strong drink may raise intense desire in the case of a drunkard. The prospect of the loss of a limb or of one's eyesight will cause strong emotions in any instance. The rapidity of the rise of an internally initiated emotion will be due to the amount of pleasure or pain, immediate or remote, which the idea suggests. As attention declines, the idea grows weaker, and the emotion begins to subside. Any idea which suggests gratification of desire, any idea which vividly pictures something affecting the welfare of the self or others, is apt to be followed by emotion. Probably no one can even imagine a person in a burning car, or lying helpless with broken limbs on a lonely road, without feeling the emotion of pity arise. To repress certain trains of feeling, repress the ideas that give them birth. This will have a restraining power, even where the emotional state tends to bring up a consonant idea, just as a fire may suggest the idea of putting fuel on it."

To sum up: Inasmuch as it is a psychological fact that ideas not only cause feelings, emotions, and desires, but also tend to revive the same, and to deepen, strengthen and nourish them, it follows that if one wishes to inhibit, repress or weaken any disadvantageous feeling, emotion, or desire, he should studiously and insistently refrain from allowing his attention to dwell upon the ideas tending to arouse or stimulate such feelings, emotions, or desires. He should refuse to feed the feeling, emotion or desire with the nourishing food of associated ideas. Instead he should set to work to starve out the objectionable feeling, emotion, or desire by refusing it the mental food needed for its nourishment and growth.

The essence, then, of the above is: "Don't feed a feeling, emotion, or desire with the nourishing and stimulating food of associated ideas; but, instead, starve out the objectionable thing by denying and refusing it such food.

4. Cultivate the Opposite. It is a law of psychology that one set of feelings, emotions, or desires may be weakened, repressed, and controlled by a careful and determined cultivation of the opposite set of feelings, emotions, or desires. Every mental state in the emotional field has its opposite state. The two states are antagonistic, and each tends to annihilate the other. The two cannot exist together at the same time and place. One cannot feel happy and miserable at the same time and place. Consequently, there is always a struggle between opposing sets of mental states if both sets have obtained a lodgment in the mental field of the individual. Everyone will readily see when the matter is thus presented to him, that if the individual, by means of the will, will throw the weight of his attention into the side of the balance in which rests the preferred set of feelings, emotions, or desires, the victory will be won for that side.

It is true that one, by a continued series of acts of sheer will, may be able to directly "kill out" an objectionable mental state of this kind—but the effort is a tremendous one, and one which is beyond the power of most persons. But, by the

Cultivation of the Opposites, the person takes advantage of the fight already under way between the two opposing emotional armies, and instead of fighting the battle all alone by a frontal attack, he forms an alliance with the friendly army, and throws the weight of his own will in its favor—he brings up a powerful reserve force, with men, equipment, ammunition, and supplies, and thus gives to the friendly army an enormously increased advantage. One has but to consider the matter in this light, in order to see that this is the best, easiest, and quickest way to conquer the objectionable mental army.

The above statement is based upon the acknowledged psychological fact which is expressed in the axiom that: "To develop a positive quality, it is important to restrain or inhibit its opposing negative; to restrain or inhibit a negative quality, develop and encourage its opposing positive." In this axiom is contained in condensed form a whole philosophy of character-building and self-improvement. Its very simplicity causes many to fail to perceive its universal application and absolute truth. "We advise each of you to commit the said axiom to memory, and to "use it in your business" of self-development and Mental Mastery.

The essence, then, of the above is: Cultivate the

opposite set of feelings, emotions, and desires, and thus restrain, suppress, inhibit, and master the set you wish to overcome and conquer.

[Note: The feelings, emotions, and desire may be cultivated by reversing the above rules given for their suppression. In the remaining pages of this chapter, moreover, specific directions for such cultivation are given. Accordingly, this last rule must he studied in connection with the further instruction given for the cultivation of the feelings, emotions, and desires.]

How to Cultivate the Feelings, Emotions, or Desires

While we might rest content to say, regarding the Cultivation of the Feelings, Emotions, and Desires, "merely reverse the rules given for the repression thereof," we have thought it better to emphasize the positive as well as the negative phases of the Mastery of Emotions, even though we may seem to be traveling over ground already covered. At the last, one always finds the positive phase the best one to apply in practice. "While we have thought it well to give the "Don't" side careful attention, because so many need it, yet, at the same time, we personally, prefer the "Do" side in imparting instruction on this subject.

Here follow the general rules for the Cultivation, Development, and Strengthening of the Power of Feelings, Emotions, and Desires:

1. Frequently express, mentally and physically, the feeling, emotion, or desire which you wish to cultivate, develop, and strengthen.

2. Form the habit of expressing in action the feeling, emotion, or desire which you wish to cultivate, develop, or strengthen.

3. Keep before you as much as possible the idea or mental image associated with the feeling, emotion, or desire which you wish to cultivate, develop or strengthen.

4. Restrain the classes of feelings, emotions, and desires opposed to those which you wish to cultivate, develop, or strengthen.

Let us now consider each one of these rules in further detail.

1. Frequently express the positive feelings, emotions, and desires. As we have seen in the earlier part of this chapter, a feeling, emotion, or desire, is developed by the physical expression thereof, and also by the frequent repetition of the same in consciousness. The expression of

the outward physical manifestations of the inner state tends not only to add fuel to the fire of the latter, but also nourishes and strengthens it. Likewise, the frequent bringing into the field of consciousness of the feeling, emotion, or desire tends to deepen the impression, and to cause the mental state to take deep roots in the mental being of the individual.

Exercise and practice develops the emotional muscles, just as they do the physical muscles. Repetition is a potent factor in forming and strengthening mental impressions, and in the cultivation of the mental habits. Consequently, lose no fit opportunity of exercising and using the feeling, emotion, or desire that you wish to cultivate and develop. Put it through its paces on the mental track. Not only frequently bring it up into the field of consciousness by means of the fixing the attention upon the associated ideas and mental images connected with it, but also express the inner feeling in the appropriate physical expressions. If you wish to be courageous, bring up often the idea of courage, and endeavor to feel its thrill through you; and at the same time, deliberately assume the physical attitude of courage. Think of yourself as the courageous individual, and try to walk, carry yourself, and in general act like that individual. Form the correct mental picture, and then endeavor to act it out.

The idea of the physical expression is well illustrated by the following quotation from a writer on the subject, who says:

"Get control of your physical channels of expression, and master the physical expression connected with the mental state you are trying to develop. For instance, if you are trying to develop your will along the lines of Self-Reliance, Confidence, Fearlessness, etc., the first thing for you to do is to get a perfect control of the muscles by which the physical manifestations or expressions of those feelings are shown. Get control of the muscles of your shoulders, that you may throw them back manfully. Look out for the stooping attitude of lack of confidence. Then get control of the muscles by which you hold up your head, with eyes front, gazing the world fearlessly in the face. Get control of the muscles of the legs by which you will be enabled to walk firmly as the positive man should. Get control of your vocal organs, by which you may speak in the resonant, vibrant tones which compel attention and inspire respect. Get yourself well in hand physically, in order to manifest these outward forms of will, and you will clear a path for your mind-power to manifest itself—and will make the work of the will much easier."

But one must not content himself with merely experiencing the mental state, and "acting out" the physical expression. Important as these may be (and they really are very important), they must be supplemented by the actual manifestation in outward form of the inner mental state which you wish to cultivate and develop. The man referred to in the above quotation must learn to occasionally actually perform some act requiring physical or moral courage. He must exercise his mental state and will by actual use. Grow by expression and action. Do the deeds, and you will acquire the power to do still greater.

The essence, then, of the above is: Express frequently, mentally and physically, in "acting out" and actual doing, the feeling, emotion, and desire which you wish to cultivate and develop.

2. Acquire the Habit of Expression. By acquiring the Habit of Expression of the feeling, emotion, or desire which you may wish to cultivate and develop, you make a mental path or channel over which the will naturally and easily travel. Habit renders the expression "second nature." Habit is formed by exercise and repetition. Every time you express a mental state,

the easier does it become to express it again, for you have started the formation of a habit. Habit is a form of mental impression, and the oftener you sink the die of action into the soft wax of the mind, the deeper will be the impression. Ease of performance increases with habit, the latter becoming "second nature." When a habit is built, it will constitute the "line of least resistance" for you, and you will find it easy to move in that direction, and hard to move in the opposite one.

The hardest work in the voluntary establishment of an emotional habit is at the beginning. This period requires the greatest determination and "stick-to-itiveness." Here you must fight with all your might, but, the first battle once won, the after-fights are less severe, and finally degenerate into mere skirmishes. Let one endeavor to establish the habit of not-smoking or not-drinking, for instance, and he will find that three-quarters of the entire struggle will be condensed in the fight of the first week, if not indeed in that of the first day. It is hard to get started. Remember old Rip Van Winkle, who never could get started—he was always saying: "Well this drink don't count" Beware of the slips at the start, for such slips lose more for one than he can regain in a whole day of success. After you have determined to establish a habit, you must not allow even one of those early slips, for this reason. A writer has said that such slips are like the dropping of a ball of cord which one is endeavoring to wind— each drop of the ball unwinds more than many windings can replace.

The essence, then of the above is: Establish firmly the habit of expressing in action the feeling, emotion, or desire which you wish to cultivate and develop.

3. Visualize the Associated Subject or Object. It is an established principle of psychology that the mental picture of the object or subject of a feeling, emotion, or desire, when held before the mind, tends to add force, power, and vitality to the emotional state representing it. And the stronger, deeper, clearer, and more frequently repeated such a mental picture is, the stronger, deeper, and more does the emotional mental state associated with it tend to become. Feelings, emotions, and desires are fed by ideas— and the strongest kind of ideas are those taking form in clear mental pictures of the imagination or memory.

A writer has said: "The clearer the mental image of the object of desire, the greater will be the degree of desire, all else being equal. A child may be filled with discontent—it wants something, but it does not know what it wants. The child thinks of 'toys'—and it begins to want still harder. Then it sees a toy—and then its want becomes very intense. One may feel hungry, in a degree, but when he sees some particular object of taste the hunger becomes far more intense. And so it follows that if one will keep on presenting to his desire the suggestion and mental image of the object, then will the desire begin to burn more fiercely and strongly, and may be cultivated to almost any degree.

You know one may awaken desire in another in this way, by means of suggestion, and by presenting the idea or mental image of the object in conversation, or by means of pictures, etc. How many of us know to our sorrow how the "sight" of a thing of which we were not thinking at the moment has caused the fire of desire to spring up suddenly and fiercely in our minds. Therefore, visualize the object or subject of the desire you wish to develop, until you can see it quite plainly. Also visualize yourself as attaining the object of the desire, and being in possession of it. Keep this mental image with you, for it has a wonderfully stimulating effect upon the desire. Keep your mind filled with mental pictures of the thing which you wish to become a habit with you, for by so doing you are constantly adding oil to the flame of desire—and desire is the motive-power of the will."

The essence, then, of the above is: Feed your mind with the ideas, and mental pictures, of the object or subject of the feeling, emotion, or desire which you wish to cultivate and develop.

4. Restrain and Suppress the Opposites. As we have seen elsewhere in this chapter, the development of an opposite set of feelings, emotions, or desires tends to restrain, suppress, and eventually destroy any particular set of these mental states. Contrariwise, it follows that if we will studiously and determinedly restrain and suppress (by the methods already given in this chapter) the feelings, emotions, and desires opposed to those which we wish to cultivate and develop, then will the favored ones be given the best possible opportunity to nourish, grow, develop, and wax strong and vigorous. Regard the opposing set as weeds, which is allowed to grow will choke and weaken, or possibly even kill, your favorite valuable plants. And you know what you should do in such a case, of course: carefully and determinedly weed out the harmful growths—pluck them up by the roots, and cast them out of your mental garden the moment they manifest an appearance.

By resolutely refusing to permit the growth of the objectionable emotional weeds of the "opposites" in your mental garden, you greatly promote the growth of the valuable plants and fruits which you wish to cultivate and develop. Remember, there is not room in the mental garden for both of the two opposing sets of emotional qualities to thrive and flourish. It is "up to you" to determine which ones shall be the victors— which ones shall be the "fittest" to survive. The "fittest" in such cases is not always the best—rather is the one which you strengthen, stimulate, and feed, by the methods mentioned herein, or similar ones based on the same principles; and which you have protected by destroying its "opposite."

It is for each and every one of you to make the decision—and the sooner the better. The question before you is: "Shall my emotional garden bear thriving weeds, noxious and poisonous to my well-being? Or shall it, instead, bear a crop of sturdy, strong and vigorous plants and fruits, which are conducive to my well-being, strength, efficiency, and ultimate happiness? It is "up to you" to decide—and then to act.

The essence, then, of the above is: Pluck out and cast off the emotional weeds—the opposites of the feelings, emotions, and desires which you wish to cultivate.

Character-Building

It may not have occurred to the reader of the preceding pages of this chapter that in cultivating and developing the positive feelings, emotions, and desires, and in restraining and repressing the negative ones, he is really performing an important work in the direction of Character-Building. But it is a fact that in this work he is really performing the basic task of the building-up of his character.

We have seen that a man's feelings, emotions, and desires really constitute the motive-power which operates in the direction of determining the character and nature of his thoughts and actions. This being so, it is seen at once that in the emotional realm of mind is to be found the principal material of that which we call Character. Therefore, in the selection and storing-up of this basic material the man really has proceeded far in the direction of Character Building.

A man's "character" is composed of his mental qualities; and his mental qualities are largely determined by the nature, quality, and quantity of his emotional factors. The work of Character Building most always begin by the Mastery of Emotion, and this mastery is attained along the lines of control, development, stimulation, direction, and cultivation similar to those indicated in this chapter.

The person wishing to scientifically build-up his character should begin by making a list of his positive and negative qualities, placing the positive qualities in one list and the negative qualities in another list. He should be honest with himself in going over this list, and should not hesitate to mark down the qualities manifest in himself which are clearly negative and disadvantageous. Nor should he let modesty prevent his marking down those qualities possessed by himself which rightfully may be called positive and advantageous. The man should be thoroughly honest in this mental stocktaking.

Having made this mental diagnosis and inventory, the person should then set deliberately to work in the direction of repressing and restraining the negative and disadvantageous qualities found on his list, in which task he should follow some such system or method as that laid down for him in this chapter. At the same time he should pay some attention to the strengthening and stimulation of the positive and advantageous qualities found on the list. In repressing and restraining the negative and disadvantageous qualities, he should not neglect to put into effect the rule therefore which teaches how to develop the "opposites" of the negative qualities; by doing this the weeds are not only rooted out, but strong healthy valuable plants and fruits are developed in their place.

The result of such exercise, practice and work, faithfully and determinedly followed for even a short time, will be very gratifying to those making the effort; many will be surprised at the decided improvement noted. And, as we shall see as we proceed, the encouragement and development of certain kinds of desire will increase the willpower of the person so that we may make great progress in his intellectual development also. And, in this work he will have enormously developed his willpower, by exercise, use, and directed and concentrated attention.

The task of Character Building is one quite worthy for performance by the Master Mind. In fact, it is one of the first things that the developing and awakening Master Mind—the Ego— should proceed to undertake and successfully carry to a conclusion. The Master Mind can build up a character to suit its tastes and highest ambitions— providing that it will take the trouble to do so; and if it is a real Master Mind, it will take the trouble, for this end justifies the work and effort required to attain it.

The Mastery of Thought

Speaking in the figurative sense, it may be
said that the Kingdom of Mind over which the
Ego—The Mind Master, or Master Mind—rules
(or may rule if it will but assert its right and
power to rule) is composed of three grand divisions, or states, namely:

(1) Feeling; (2) Thought; and (3) Will. The
activities of the mind consist of Feeling, Thinking, and Willing. All mental states or processes
will be found to come under one or the other
of the said classes. And yet, so complex are the
mental activities, that each of these three respective classes are usually found manifesting
in connection with one or more of the others.

It is very seldom that we find a Thought without
also finding a blending of Feelings, and usually
a manifestation of Will, as well. Likewise, we
seldom find a Feeling without a Thought connected or associated with it, and usually a manifestation of the presence of Will in connection
with it. And, finally, we seldom find a manifestation of Will without the presence of Feeling,
and of the Thought associated with the Feeling.
But, nevertheless, there is a clear distinction between each of these three great classes of mental states or processes; and for the purposes of

intelligent study of them it is almost imperative that we separate the mental states and process into these three classes, that we may consider, inspect, and analyze them into the elements.

In the preceding several chapters we have considered, inspected, and analyzed the great division or class of Feeling; and we shall now proceed to treat the great division or class of Thought in the same way.

To begin with, let us ask ourselves the question, "What is Thought? What do we mean when we say that we 'think'?" Unless we have previously looked up the definition, or else have carefully considered the matter, we will find it very difficult to express in words just what we mean when we employ the terms "thought," and "to think." We are sure that we do know, but the moment that we try to express the idea in words, then we find that we do not really "know" in the full sense of the term. Let us then turn to the reference books and see just what the best authorities have to say on the subject.

We find that "Thought" is defined as: "Thinking; exercise of the mind in any of its higher forms; reflection; cogitation." And that "Thinking" is defined as: "Using the higher powers of the mind; employing the Intellect; performing

the mental, operation of apprehension, deliberation, or judgment." The above definitions (like
many others of their kind) do not help us very
much in the matter, do they? Let us seek the
opinion of the psychologists. A leading psychologist tells us that: "To think is to compare
things with each other, to notice wherein they
agree and differ, and to classify them according
to these agreements and differences. It enables
us to put into a few classes the billions of things
that strike our perceptive faculties; to the things
with like qualities into a bundle by themselves,
and to infer that what is true of one of these
things will be true of the others, without actual
experience in each individual case; and to intro-
duce law and order into what at first seemed a
mass of chaotic materials."

Another has said: "Stating the matter plainly,
we may say that Thinking is the mental process
of (1) comparing our perceptions of things with
each other; (2) Classifying them according to
their ascertained likeness or difference; and
thus tying them up in mental bundles with each
set of "things of a kind" in its own bundle; (3)
forming the abstract, symbolic mental idea (or
"concept") of each class of things, so grouped,
which we may afterward use just as we use
figures in mathematical calculations; (4) using these "concepts" in order to form "infer-

ences"; that is, to reason from the known to the unknown, and to form judgments regarding things; (5) comparing these judgments and deducing higher judgments from them, and so on.

Many of us who are unfamiliar with the subject, will be surprised to know that they have been performing all of these several kinds of mental operations all their life, without knowing that they did so. They are like the man who when told the difference between poetry and prose, exclaimed: ''Well, just to think of it! Here I have been talking and writing 'prose' all my life, and I never knew it!" But the thinking mind really performs all of the several mental operations as a matter of everyday routine, without realizing the different stages. Just as you never realize or are conscious of the various distinct muscular actions you perform in the ordinary act of walking, so you are unconscious of the various mental actions you perform in the ordinary act of thinking; but in both cases you do perform the action, even though you may be unconscious of the mechanism employed therein.

And it is through this wonderful series of processes, built upon degrees of perfection as the race has evolved, that Man, even from the beginning has worked his way up from a position which was little above that of the higher beasts, to that of the mastery of the living creatures, and to the partial mastery of Nature, herself. And in the saint: way the Man of the future—the Man of the Master Mind, will evolve into a position as much higher than that of the average man of today as that of the latter is higher than that of his humble ancestor of the cave-dwelling and stone-age days. We are so accustomed to taking things for granted that we fail to appreciate the long road that man has traveled to attain his present position of intellectual supremacy, or the terrible struggles he has had along the road. The following quotation from a leading writer on the subject will perhaps give us a clearer understanding of just what Thought has meant, and has accomplished for Man; and also what it may have in store for the race in the future—and for the individual HERE and NOW who will attain the Mastery of Mind by becoming a Master Mind.

The writer in question says: ''Nature is constantly using her power to kill off the thoughtless, or to cripple them in life's race. She is determined that only the fittest and the descendants of the fittest shall survive. By the 'fittest' she means those who have thought and whose ancestors have thought and profited thereby.

"Geologists tell us that ages ago there lived in England bears, tigers, elephants, lions, and many other powerful and fierce animals. There was living contemporaneous with them a much weaker animal, that had neither the claws, the strength, nor the speed of the tiger. In fact, this human being was almost defenseless. Had a being from another planet been asked to prophesy, he would undoubtedly have said that this helpless animal would be the first to be exterminated. And yet every one of those fierce creatures succumbed either to the change of the climate, or to man's inferior strength. The reason was that man had one resource denied to the animals—the power of progressive thought.

"The land sank, the sea cut off England from the mainland, the climate changed, and even the strongest animals were helpless. But man changed his clothing with the changing climate. He made fires; he built a retreat to keep off death by cold. He thought out means to kill or to subdue the strongest animals. Had the lions, tigers or bears the power of progressive thought, they could have combined, and it would have been possible for them to exterminate Man before he reached the civilized stage.

"Man no longer sleeps in caves. The smoke no longer fills his home or finds its way out through the chinks in the walls or a hole in the roof. In traveling, he is no longer restricted to his feet or even to horses. For all this improvement Man is indebted to Thought."

And, continuing the same line of thought, it may be seen in the imagination how much further Man is clearly destined to proceed on the ascending path that leads to the mountain top of attainment. He has not only even now mastered the face of the earth, but has gone far toward the mastery of the seas and the depths under the seas; and is now well on his way to the mastery of the air as well. He has harnessed the forces of Nature, proceeding from the grosser to the fined—from steam to electricity—and still has a far more wonderful field to explore in the world of forces still finer than that of electricity.

It is said that in a single square foot of the air there is contained sufficient atomic power (if once released and transmitted to machinery) to run the entire machinery of the earth for many years! And, beyond that is the still finer forces of the ether, the power of which are almost incalculable.

Man is rapidly evolving from the plane of physical power on to that of mental power. The man of the future will be as a super-man compared to the men of today. He will use the powers of his mind so as to make the whole of Nature his slave. The individuals of the Master Mind are the forerunners of these Supermen. Even now, they are mastering adverse conditions by the powers of Thought; and day by day, year by year, the boundaries of the Unknown are receding before the Master Minds of the race, and their boundaries of their Mental Kingdom are spreading out before them in a wondrous progression. This, of all the ages of Man, is the Age of Thought! Surely the view is enticing and tempting to the awakening Ego. Here then, reader, is the work before you—the Mastery of Thought. You are invited to consider the principles of this wondrous attainment, and to proceed to the practical demonstration thereof.

Many persons believe that they are "thinking" when they are but exercising their faculty of memory, and that in merely an idle and passive manner. They are simply allowing the stream of memory to flow through their field of consciousness, while the Ego stands on the banks and idly watches the passing waters of memory flow by. They call this "thinking," while in reality there is no process of Thought under way. Some of these persons remind one of the old story of the man who when asked what he was doing when he sat so silently and quietly on the

fence rail of the old fence; the old man. reply-
ing, "Waal, sometimes I sit and think, and other
times I just sit."

A writer has said of this confusion of ideas:
"Thinking means a variety of things. You may
have looked out of your train window while
passing a field, and it may have occurred to you
that that field would make an excellent baseball
diamond. Then you 'thought' of the time when
you played baseball, 'thought' of some particular game perhaps, 'thought' how you had made
a grand stand play or a bad muff, and how one
day it began to rain in the middle of the game,
and the team took refuge in the carriage shed.
Then you 'thought' of other rainy days rendered
particularly vivid for some reason or other,
or perhaps your mind came back to considering, and how long it was going to last. And of
course, in one sense you were 'thinking.'

"But when I use the word 'thinking,' I mean
thinking with a purpose, with an end in view,
thinking to solve a problem. I mean the kind of
thinking that is forced on us when we are deciding on a course to pursue, on a life work you
take up perhaps: the kind of thinking that was
forced upon us in our younger days when we
had to find a solution to a problem in mathemat-
ics, or when we tackled psychology in college.

I do not mean 'thinking' in snatches, or holding petty opinions on this subject and on that. I mean thought on significant questions which lie outside the bounds of your narrow personal welfare. This is the kind of thinking which is now so rare—so badly needed!

"The term 'thinking' is loosely used to cover a wide range of mental processes. These processes we may roughly divide into Memory, Imagination, and Reasoning. It is the last only with which we have to deal. I admit that development of the memory is desirable. I admit that development of the imagination is equally desirable. But, by 'thinking,' I mean Reasoning."

The same writer has well said: "Modern psychologists tell us that all Reasoning begins in perplexity, hesitation, doubt. It is essential that we keep this in mind, it differs from the popular conception even more than may appear at first sight. If a man were to know everything, he could not think. Nothing would ever puzzle him, his purposes would never be thwarted, he would never experience perplexity or doubt, he would have no problems. Were we to study the origin and evolution of thinking, we would doubtless find that thinking arose in just this way—from thwarted purposes. If our lives and the lives of our ancestors had always run smoothly, if our every desire were immediately satisfied, if we never met an obstacle in anything we tried to do, thinking would never have appeared on this planet. But adversity forced us to it."

Let us now consider the various stages of the mental process or processes that are involved in the activities that we call Thinking.

Analysis. The logicians tell us that the first step in the process of Reasoning is that of comparing one thing with another, for the purpose of discovering points of difference or likeness, and for the further purpose of classification according to those likenesses or differences. But in order to compare different things we must first have observed them and discovered their respective qualities; for the difference in things arises solely by reason of the difference in the qualities of the respective things. And, in order to discover the qualities of things, we must pursue the process of analysis.

Analysis means: "An examination of the component parts of anything, whether an object of the senses or of the intellect, for the purpose of reducing that thing into its original elements."

Everything that is known to us in conscious

experience is found to be composed and made up of certain "qualities." These qualities constitute the "characteristics" of the thing, and make the thing just what it is as distinguished from other things. We cannot think of a thing without qualities, and if we try to abstract the qualities from a thing, and then set aside these abstracted qualities, we find that we have nothing left of the thing. One perception of, or our representative idea of, any object is simply a perception or represented idea of the various qualities which we have discovered in the thing; this because the object itself is merely a composite of these qualities, at least so far as its perception in our consciousness is concerned.

We may realize the above fact more clearly if we apply it to some concrete and specific object. Take a horse, for instance: try to think of the horse without reference to its several qualities, properties, and attributes, and you will find that you have no distinct, idea of anything that can be known in consciousness—you have merely a name left, and nothing else, and the horse itself has disappeared. Or, take a rose: try to think of a rose without considering its color, its odor, its shape, its size, its response to touch, etc., and you have left simply the name of the rose. And this rule applies to anything and everything which we may know, or seek to know, in conscious experience.

This being so, it follows that in order to know anything, we must know what it is; and this "what-it-is" is known only by combining our knowledge of its several qualities perceived by us. And in order to know these several qualities, we must apply Perception in the direction of Analysis.

It is astonishing to most of us to discover how little really we know about the most common objects about us when we try to set down on paper a list of the qualities which we have discovered in the objects. Like the student of Agassiz, in the story told in a preceding chapter, we find that "what we don't know would fill a book." The cultivation of Perception will, of course, greatly increase our knowledge of the objects of our consideration.

Some good teachers have held that the best way of imparting instruction to pupils is that of asking them questions concerning the subject under consideration. This does not mean merely the asking of formal questions taken from a book, but questions designed to bring out the knowledge already in the minds of the pupil, and the further knowledge to be developed by the process of thought on the part of the pupil which are set in motion by the question. A writer has said of this plan:

"The questions should be asked for the purpose of unfolding their minds, and to teach them to lay up their knowledge in a natural and regular way. The questions should be asked in the form of general conversation, and not taken from books. The questions will be found to spring naturally out of the pupil's preceding answers, and should be asked as nearly as possible in his own words—the principle of similarity guiding the whole. Socrates, Plato, and others among the ancients, and some moderns, have been masters of this art. The principle of asking questions and obtaining answers to them may be said to characterize all intellectual effort. The child makes its first entrance into the field of knowledge by asking questions, and the crowning efforts of the philosopher are still asking questions and attempting to find answers to them. The great thing is to ask the right questions and to obtain the right answers."

Socrates, the ancient philosopher, was an adept in this form of extracting knowledge from the mind of his pupils and others with whom he came in contact. In fact, the method has since been known as "The Socratic Method." Socrates compared himself to the midwife assisting in the birth of a child, and claimed that the process of the birth of ideas was assisted by his method of intelligent questioning. Dr. Hodgson, in the last century, was a modern adept in the same method. His biographer has said: "This art of questioning possessed by him was something wonderful and unique, and was to the mind of most of his pupils a truly obstetric art. He told them little or nothing, but showed them how to find out by themselves. He said that the Socratic method was the true one, especially with the young."

Just as the student is assisted in the discovery of knowledge in his own mind concerning things, so is any person assisted in the same way by asking himself questions concerning "what do I know about this thing," and by the additional search made by the person in response to his discovery of how little he knows about the thing in question. But this self-questioning must be done logically, and intelligently, and not in a mere haphazard manner. A writer has said regarding this: "In proposing questions it is very necessary to keep in view the importance of arranging them in the exact order in which the subject would naturally develop itself in the mind of a logical and systematic thinker."

Many systems of extracting knowledge concerning subjects or objects have been devised by different teachers of the subject. The same general principle underlies them all. The following, known as "The Seven Questions," has been highly recommended by some careful students of the subject. Here the following Seven Questions are asked oneself concerning a subject or object under consideration:

1. Who?

2. Which?

Return to top

3. What?

4. When?

5. Where?

Return to top

6. Why?

7. How?

In the "Seven Questions," we find that the first two questions bring out and establish the identity of the subject or object; the third brings out the action to or by the thing; the fourth and fifth, the place and time; the sixth, the reason or purpose; and the seventh, the manner of the action. It will be found that this apparently simple code of questions will bring out a wealth of detail regarding any subject, object, person, thing, or event.

A somewhat more complex method is mentioned in my work on "Memory Training," and has been used by me in my personal class work. It is as follows:

1. What is the name of this thing?

2. When did (or does) it exist?

3. Where did (or does) it exist?

4. What caused it to exist?

5. What is its history?

6. What are its leading characteristics?

7. What is its use and purpose?

8. What are its effects, or results

9. What does it prove or demonstrate?

10. What is its probable end or future?

11. What does it most resemble?

12. What are its opposites (things most unlike it)?

13. What do I know about it, generally, in the way of associated ideas?

14. What is my general opinion regarding it?

15. What degree of interest has it for me?

16. What are my general feelings regarding it—degree of like or dislike?

This system will bring out of your mind a surprising volume of information. Try it occasionally, and you will perceive its possibilities and degree of usefulness.

Comparison. The second stage of Reasoning is that of Comparison, i.e., of the process of comparing one thing, or class of things, with another—this for the purpose of discovering points of likeness or difference, which process will result in that of classification, a later stage. As we have seen, the process of Comparison must be preceded by that of Analysis, for we compare things only by comparing their respective qualities, and we discover these qualities only by the process of analysis of some kind of degree.

So important are the elementary process of thinking that some authorities have held that Thinking may be said to be composed of Analysis, Comparison, and Classification, the rest being but modifications or extensions of these elementary mental processes.

In Analysis we find that a thing has many characteristics, i.e., qualities, properties, or attributes. Then, by Comparison, we discover that other things (previously analyzed) have characteristics differing in kind or degree from those of the first thing. When the characteristics of two or more things are near in kind or degree, we say that the things are "like" each other. When we find that these respective characteristics are far apart in degree or kind, we say that they are "unlike" each other.

Philosophers have sought to group qualities into "pairs or opposites," it being held that each quality has necessarily an opposite quality or "contradictory." Thus we have hard and soft, high and low, wide and narrow, large and small, straight and crooked, up and down, far and near, etc.

The tendency to associate things according to "likeness" manifests itself at a very low scale in human development, and is one of the first manifestations of the reasoning process in the mind of the young child. Many of these points of "likeness," however, are afterward discovered to be merely superficial. For instance, the guinea-pig is no pig at all, its name being given merely because its general shape resembled that of the pig. Again, a whale is commonly regarded as a fish, whereas it is not a fish at all, but is a warm-blooded animal, suckling its young—it is much more like a seal than like a fish, although its outer appearance is like that of the fish, and the fact that it lives in the water added to the first impression. Again, to the small child a lion or bear is a "big dog," and a cow is "a horse with horns."

Similarly, egg-plants obtain their name because of their formal resemblance to the egg; peanuts, because they are contained in a pod as are peas. Lamps originally were torches, and when a wick-burning vessel was employed as a substitute for the torchlamp the old name was retained. Similarly, we now speak of an "electric lamp," merely because the electric apparatus gives light as did the oil-lamp, or its predecessor the original torch-lamp.

It has been said that, in a way, the perception of "likeness" is to an extent, the perception of "unlikeness." In other words, if we did not recognize the existence of the "opposite" quality we would not recognize the first one. For instance, if all things were "straight" we would not have our attention called to "straightness" as a quality— we would take the condition for granted and would not think of it at all. If we dwelt in a region of perpetual daylight, we would not think of "daylight" or "daytime" at all; but as soon as we recognize the opposite or contrasting condition, i.e., that of "darkness" or "nighttime," we recognize the existence of "daylight" or "daytime." In short, we recognize a quality only when the "different thing" presents itself to us.

Experience, however, has given the race the almost intuitive and instinctive realization of "the pairs of opposites," or "contradictories." So true is this that the trained mind instinctively leaps to the thought of an "opposite" at the same time that it is considering any given quality. It thinks of this "opposite" not because of its "likeness" to the thing under consideration, but because of its "un-likeness" or difference. So true is this that psychologists hold that we can obtain a clearer and more distinct idea or mental image of anything if we will at the same time think of its "opposite"—either its opposite quality, or a thing whose qualities are markedly opposite to that of the thing under consideration. In associating a thing with others in our memory, or thought, we do so by (1) association with "like" things, and (2) by association with "unlike" ones. The greater the "likeness" the greater is the strength and value of the first form of association; and the greater the "unlikeness" the greater is the strength and value of the second form.

A very warm place is remembered easily in connection with another very warm place; or, equally well, in connection with a very cold place. Mention a celebrated giant, and the mind first recalls the idea of other giants, and then flies to the other extreme and thinks of celebrated dwarfs. A very fat man suggests (a) other fat men, and (b) very thin men. In the above cases we find that the memory does not recall men of average stature or average weight. What is said here regarding the tendency of the memory is also true concerning the processes of general thought.

The most common points of Comparison, for the purpose of discovering "likeness" and "un-likeness," are as follows: Name; Place; Time; Shape; Cause; Effect; Use; Actions; General Idea or Character; History; Origin; and Destination. Apply your test of Comparison along the lines of each of the above mentioned points concerning the things being compared by you, and you will build up a strong web of associations which will hold fast your thought and memory concerning the respective things. The more associations you have concerning a thing, the better will you "know" that thing.

Classification. The third stage of Reasoning is that of Classification, of the process of "tying in bundles" of thought and association the things which resemble each other, so as to be reason concerning these numerous separate things afterward. The process of Classification is of course opposite to that of Analysis; the first consists of taking apart the qualities of things for the purpose of examination, while the second consists of putting together things for the purpose of reasoning about them. Classification is also often spoken of as Generalization.

It is a fundamental principle of psychology that several distinct things may be associated in memory, and in the reasoning processes, by

reason of their having been grouped into logical and natural classes, families, divisions, etc.
This process is akin to that of placing together
in the same compartment, drawer, or envelope,
the things which are "alike" each other. The
receptacle is also generally found immediately
adjoining one containing the things as nearly
opposite in character as possible—each set of
things being classified in direct contrast with its
opposite. This fact being perceived, it will also
be seen that the man of trained intellect will
be found to have acquired the habit of careful
classification and generalization. This mental
characteristic, by the way, is almost invariably
possessed by persons of the scientific type of
mind—not only those engaged in the ordinary
scientific pursuits, but also the efficient individuals in the professions, trades, and branches of
business. The efficient man in any walk of life
is usually found to have acquired the scientific
habit of classification, grouping of ideas, and
mental-filling methods.

A writer has said concerning this: "The man
who has not properly classified the myriad individual objects with which he has to deal, must
advance like a cripple. He only can travel with
seven league boots, who has thought out the
relations existing between these stray individual
objects, and put them into their proper classes.

In a minute, a business man may put his hand upon any one of ten thousand letters, if they are properly classified. In the same way, the student of any branch can, if he studies the subjects aright, have all his knowledge classified and speedily available for use."

All students, or persons desiring to master any subject in the field of intellectual endeavor, will find their work immensely improved, and their efficiency enormously increased, if they will make a written chart or diagram of any subject with which they wish to familiarize themselves, placing each important division of the idea in its proper place, and in its proper and logical relation to other divisions. The mind will then take up the arrangement of such chart or diagram, and will follow the same in its thought-processes, and in its memory-processes. The preacher or lawyer does this in his preparation of sermons or briefs, and often actually "sees" these divisions and classifications in his "mind's eye" when he begins to speak, and all through his discourse. The efficient sales-man does the same thing, and thus gets the best result of his work. Efficiency in almost any line of work depends materially upon this "diagramming" of the items of knowledge which have been acquired in the experience and study of the person.

Classification should begin with the most general, and broadest classification, and then proceed to the more particular and more limited ones. The more general and broader class will of course contain the greatest number of individual items of thought; and as the classification narrows itself, the number of the individual items of course lessens. An example of scientific classification is had in the method of indexing followed in the large libraries. Go to some large library, and you will find that each and every general class of boots has its general class number—it is in the 100 class, or the 200 class, or the 900 class, and so on. Then these "hundreds" are subdivided into sections, numbered 1, 2, 3, 4, 5, 6, etc.

Then comes a closer subdivision, and so on until finally it comes down to the individual books, each of which it has its own special number which cannot be rightly had by any other book in the library. Under this system, it is possible for a person familiar with it to go to the shelves of any library using the same system, and there pick out any one particular book of the many thousands on its shelves—even though he had never been inside of that particular library before. He would first go to the shelf numbered in the "hundred" that he wanted, then he would find the right subdivision, and then the minor subdivision, and so on until the particular book is found. And, note this fact, the book would be found in the one particular small place where it belonged—and this particular place is the only possible place in which it could be found. And, finally, just as this particular book had only one proper place in which to be, and as each particular name in a card-index system has only one possible place in which to be, so in a well classified mind there is a certain place—a one possible place—in which a certain mental fact is to be found, and where it will always be found. By knowing this place, the thing can always be found.

A writer has said: "We classify things together whenever we observe that they are like each other in any respect, and therefore think of them together. In classifying a collection of objects, we do not merely put together in groups those which resemble each other, but we also divide each class into smaller ones in which the resemblance is more complete. Thus, the class of white substances may be divided into those which are solid, and those which are fluid, so that we get the two minor classes of solid-white and fluid-white substances. It is desirable to have names by which to show that one class is contained in another, and, accordingly, we call the class which is divided into two or more smaller ones the genus, and the smaller ones into which it is divided, the species." Every species then, is seen to be a small collection of the particular individuals composing it, and at the same time the species is an individual species of the genus of which it is a part; likewise, the genus, while a family of several species, is at the same time an individual genus to the greater family or genus of which it forms a part.

Another writer has said: "The student may familiarize himself with the principle of Generalization by considering himself as an individual named "John Smith." John represents the primary unit of generalization. The next step is to combine John with the other Smiths of his immediate family. Then that family may be grouped with his near blood relations, and so on, until finally all the related Smiths, near and remote, are grouped together in a great Smith Family. Then, the family group may be enlarged until it takes in all the white people in a county, then all the white people in the State, then all in the United States; then all the white races, then all the white and other colored skinned races, then all Mankind. Then, if one is inclined, the process may be continued until it embraces every living creature from Moneron to Man.

"Then, reversing the process, living creatures may be divided and subdivided until all mankind is seen to stand as a grand class. Then the race of mankind may be divided into sub-races according to color; then the white race may be divided into Americans and non-Americans. Then the Americans may be divided into inhabitants of the several States, or else into Indians and non-Indians; then into the inhabitants of Indians; then into the inhabitants of Posey County, Indiana. The Posey County people may be divided into Smiths and non-Smiths; then the Smith family into its constituent family groups, and then into smaller families, and so on, until at last the classification terminates in one particular John Smith who is found to be an individual, and in a class by himself."

Conception. By Conception (as used in this connection) is meant, "That act of mind by which it forms an idea of a class; or that enables the mind to correctly use general names. A "concept" is: "A general idea concerning a general class of things." As for example: the terms dog, cat, man, horse, houses, etc., each represent and expresses some concept or general idea of a class of things.

The mind forms a concept in the following manner: (1) It perceives a number of things;

then (2) it observes certain qualities possessed by those things; then (3) it compares the several qualities of the respective things which it has perceived; then (4) it classifies those things according to their discovered likeness and unlikeness; then

(5) it forms a general idea of ''concept'' embodying each certain class of things, and it usually gives to such concept a name, the latter being known as its "term."

For instance, after perceiving, observing, and classifying a number of a certain kind of four-footed animals, and finding certain basic points of "likeness" underlying their particular "unlikeness," the mind forms a concept, or class-idea, of that class of animals, and then gives to that class or concept the term or name of "dog." Now please note that this concept and term, "dog" not only embraces every one of the different individual dogs, but also all the different classes or breeds of dogs. Underlying all of the individual differences, and the differences between the several breeds, there is a common "dog-ness" belonging to all the individuals and breeds— the common quality, or set of qualities, makes a dog a dog, and entitles him to a place in the great dog family.

Now note another important fact: while you have a very clear mental concept of "dog," you cannot have a clear mental picture of "dog." While your concept embraces all dogs, yet your mental picture is necessarily limited to one particular dog—you cannot mentally picture an animal combining all the different qualities of all the individual dogs: you cannot picture a composite dog embracing all the qualities of the greyhound, the bulldog, the mastiff, the poodle, the toy-terrier, etc., all in one picture. Yet your concept includes and embraces all of these. The concept really means ''all dog,'' and you cannot make a mental picture of "all dog," for no such creature exists outside of the intellectual realm. The concept, then, and the term expressing it, is seen to be like an algebraic or geometrical symbol, inasmuch as it "stands for" certain things not mentally pictured. It is like the figure "4" which stands for "four of anything."

In addition to the concepts of classes of concrete objects, we form abstract concepts denoting classes of qualities. For instance, we have the following abstract concepts, viz., Sweetness, Hardness, Courage, Energy, Beauty, etc., none of which represent a concrete object, but each of which represents a certain quality considered as a class. "Sweetness" is not a concrete object, but merely a concept of a certain general class of quality found in things.

A writer says of this class of concepts: "Color, shape, size, mental qualities, habits of action— these are some of the qualities first observed in things and abstracted from them in thought. Redness, sweetness, hardness, softness, large- ness, smallness, fragrance, swiftness, slowness, fierceness, gentleness, warmth, cold—these are abstracted qualities of things. Of course these qualities are really never divorced from things, but the mind divorces them in order to make thinking easier. The process of converting qualities into concepts is performed simply by transforming adjective terms into their corre- sponding noun terms, and then employing each thought represented by each term as a symbol to express that particular class of quality. For instance, a piece of colored candy possesses the qualities of being round, hard, sweet, red, etc. Transforming these adjectives of quality into noun terms we have the concepts of roundness, hardness, redness, and sweetness, respectively; and we then use each of the latter as a symbol in denoting that particular class of qualities wherever it is found."

Another writer has said, on the same subject: "Our dictionaries contain such words as purity, sweetness, whiteness, industry, courage. No one ever touched, tasted, smelled, heard, or saw purity or courage. We do not, therefore, gain our knowledge of those through the senses. We have seen pure persons, pure honey; we have breathed pure air, tasted pure coffee. From all these different objects we have abstracted the only like quality, the quality of being pure. We then say we have an idea of 'purity,' and that idea is an abstract one. No one ever saw whiteness. He may have seen white clouds, snow, cloth, blossoms, houses, paper, horses, but he never saw 'whiteness' by itself. He simply abstracted that quality from various white objects."

Each concrete concept consists of a bundle of abstract concepts denoting general qualities. The concrete concept "dog" contains within itself all the qualities common to all dogs. The rule is that "Each class concept must contain within itself as many abstract concepts of quality as are common to the class represented by the concrete concept."

The processes of Analysis, Comparison, Classification, and Conception, respectively, depend for their value upon the strength and keenness of Perception attained by the application of Voluntary Attention. And Voluntary Attention, as we have seen, is an act of Will, under the direct control of the Ego. Thus, we see that the Master Mind has a part of its work these processes concerned with Thought. And, as we shall presently discover, the value of our Thought depends largely upon the correctness of our Concepts, it follows that the Master Mind has in his control the very springs from which the streams of Thought emerge and flow.

Real thinking is a process directly under the control, direction, and management of the Master Mind, from start to finish. The importance of this fact can be correctly estimated only when one realizes the all important part played by Thought in the life and welfare of the individual. "As a man thinketh, so is he." "We are the result of what we have thought." The Master Mind thinks what it wills to think, not what others will it to think, or what Chance determines it shall think. Thus is the Master Mind the Master of Itself.

In the next chapter we shall take up our consideration of the processes of Thought, beginning at this point where we are considering the nature of the Concept, and the Process of Conception.

Mastery of Reasoning

We have seen that a Concept expresses our general idea of a class of things. And, as we shall presently see, our idea of a particular object is frequently derived by Deductive Reasoning from our class concepts, it follows that our knowledge concerning any particular thing is largely obtained through our concept of the class to which the thing belongs—or rather, from the classes to which it belongs, for every concrete thing belongs to a number of classes. This being seen, it is perceived that it is of the highest importance that we form accurate and full concepts regarding the classes of things which are concerned with our chosen field of knowledge.

We have seen that the concept of a class of concrete objects must of necessity include all the qualities common to that class. But it does not, and can not, also include any of the qualities which pertain only to certain individuals or groups within the general class. For example: the concept "dog" must include all the qualities or characteristics common to all dogs. But it cannot include any of the qualities or characteristics which are possessed only by some dogs, and not by others. Thus, the concept "dog" cannot include the qualities of color, particular shape, curl of tail, shape of head, etc., for such would not be true of all dogs. But, likewise, no one of the general qualities which distinguish all dogs, and which in combination constitute the "dogness" of the animal, can be absent from the concept, if the latter is accurate, complete, and full.

As a consequence of the above, it is seen that (1) the larger the number of individual things in a class represented by a concept, the smaller must be the general qualities included in that concept; and (2) the larger the number of general qualities included in a concept, the smaller must be the number of the individuals in the class represented by the concept. For instance, the large number of individual dogs included in the general concept "dog" is in marked contrast to the small number of individual dogs included in the sub-class concept "bull-dog," or "toy-terrier," or "beagle-hound," respectively. It will be seen, of course, that the general concept really includes all the individuals of any of the sub-classes, and of all other sub-classes of dogs as well—yet each of the sub-classes has a large list of essential qualities, while the general class has only comparatively few qualities.

Here is the whole thing in a nutshell: "The greater the number of individuals, the smaller the number of class qualities; the smaller the number of individuals, the greater the number of class qualities." The single individual, of course, has a greater number of qualities that can any sub-class or general class of which he is a unit; and any general class, of course, has a smaller number of general qualities than can any sub-class or individuals included in it. The individual is "in a class by himself," and all of his qualities are general qualities. As a writer has said: "The secret is this: No two individuals can have as many qualities in common as each has individually, unless they are both precisely alike in every respect, which is impossible in nature."

Our concept of a thing expresses our knowledge of that thing. Think over this statement for a moment, for it is important. It being accepted as correct, it follows that our knowledge of a thing is wrapped up in one concept of it, and that if our concept is deficient or imperfect, or erroneous, then our knowledge of the thing must be likewise. You may think that the concept of every person concerning the same thing must be identical, but the contrary is found to be the fact. You may test this by asking a number of persons to state their "notion" (i.e., concept) of the following things, viz., Love, Faith, God, Duty, Phosphorus, Carbon. You will find that nearly every person will express a different notion concerning these general ideas.

A writer says: "My idea or image is mine alone—the reward of careless observation if imperfect; of attentive, careful, and varied observation if correct. Between mine and yours a great gulf is fixed. No man can pass from mine to yours, or from yours to mine. Neither in any proper sense of the term can mine be conveyed to you. Words do not convey thoughts; they are not vehicles of thoughts in any true sense of that term. A word is merely a common symbol which each person associates with his own idea or image."

We frequently find that when a person disagrees with our notion concerning a thing, he may be "thinking of something else"—something entirely different. Men frequently quarrel and engage in disputes because they fail to observe the old adage: "Define your terms before you dispute regarding them." The writer says: "It must be borne in mind that most of our concepts are subject to change during our entire life; that at first they are made only in a tentative way; that experience may show us, at any time, that they have been erroneously formed, that we have abstracted too little or too much, made a class too wide or too narrow, or that here a quality must be added or there one taken away."

The student will find a great help in forming correct, adequate, and full concepts in the form of a good dictionary, and, if possible, also in the form of a good encyclopedia. Reference to the dictionary, or the encyclopedia, will dispel many erroneous concepts, and improve, correct, and fill out many imperfect or incomplete ones. Your concept of a thing is your answer to the question: "What do I understand this thing to be."

The absolutely complete and full concept would necessarily include all the essential qualities thereof, with no non-essential quality. But inasmuch as no person can be held to possess absolute knowledge about anything, it follows that no absolute concepts are possessed by anyone—the best that anyone can do is to have a full, complete, perfect, and correct concept as is possible. And education, investigation, research, and experience are constantly adding to the fullness and correctness of our concepts. A well-known authority has given us a number of excellent examples of this fact, of which the following illustrations are drawn: When to our concept of a certain kind of three-leaved ivy we add the quality of "poisonous," we make a most important addition. When we add to our concept of a certain kind of fruit the quality of "good food," we have gained an important bit of practical knowledge. When we add to our concept of mustard the quality of "an antidote for opium poisoning," we have acquired valuable knowledge which may save our life at some time in the future. When men added to their concept of a certain hard, black, stony substance the attribute or quality of "burning and producing heat," they made a great discovery—and it took men many centuries to discover this. When men added to their concept of "electricity" the quality of "usable energy," and a like quality to their concept of "steam," the world's progress was added to.

The writer in question says regarding this: "Judgment is the power revolutionizing the world. The revolution is slow because nature's forces are so complex, so hard to be reduced to their simplest forms and so disguised and neutralized by the presence of other forces. The progress of the next hundred years will join many concepts, which now seem to have no common qualities. Fortunately, judgment is ever silently working and comparing things that, to past ages, have seemed dissimilar; and it is continually abstracting and leaving out of the field those qualities which have simply served to obscure the point at issue."

Reasoning. By Reasoning, man is enabled to take a short cut to knowledge of particular things. If we had to examine each particular object in order to find out its general qualities, we would make but little progress in knowledge. Life would be far too short for us to gain much knowledge about the world in which we live, and about ourselves. Here Reasoning presents itself as a short cut to such knowledge—a formula by means of which we may acquire knowledge from general principles, and apart from special investigation in each and every instance.

Reasoning is the process whereby we ascertain new knowledge from old knowledge. An authority defines it as: "The act of going from the unknown to the known through other beliefs; of basing judgment upon judgment; of basing new beliefs upon old beliefs." Reasoning is generally classified as follows: (1) Reasoning by Analogy; (2) Reasoning by Induction; and (3) Reasoning by Deduction. We shall now present to you the general characteristics of each of these classes.

Reasoning by Analogy. This is the simplest form of reasoning. It is based upon the general principle that: "If two things resemble each other in many points, they will probably resemble each other in more points." This form of reasoning differs only in degree from the process (previously considered by us) known as Classification or Generalization. The latter process proceeds upon the principle that "when many things resemble each other in a few basic qualities, we associate them in a class, and use the class-concept in further reasoning." In Reasoning by Analogy, however, the principle may be said to be that "when a few things resemble each other in many qualities, it is a case of analogy, and is used in further reasoning on that basis."

Reasoning by Analogy is the most popular form of reasoning, and perhaps the most liable to error. While very useful for ordinary purposes, one must always be on guard against error in judgment in such reasoning, for this form of reasoning has a large percentage of error. As a writer says: "Persons have been poisoned by toadstools by reason of false analogous reasoning that because mushrooms are edible, then toadstools, which resemble them, must also be fit for food; or in the same way, because certain berries resemble other edible berries they must likewise be good food. A complete analysis and classification, in these cases, would have prevented the erroneous analogy." Another writer says: "To infer that because John Smith has a red nose and is also a drunkard, then Henry Jones, who also has a red nose, is also a drunkard, would be dangerous inference. Conclusions of this kind drawn from Analogy are frequently dangerous." Another writer says: "Many false analogies are manufactured, and it is excellent thought training to expose them. The majority of people think so little that they swallow these false analogies just as newly-fledged robins swallow small stones dropped into their mouths."

If we pursue our Reasoning by Analogy far enough, however, and along the lines of logical thought, we really begin to employ Inductive Reasoning and Deductive Reasoning, and thus no longer can be said to be employing simple Reasoning by Analogy. This statement will be more clearly perceived as we consider the higher forms of reasoning above referred to. These two forms of higher reasoning are as follows: (1) Reasoning by Induction, or "inference from particular facts to general laws"; and (2) Reasoning by Deduction, or "inference from general truths to particular truths." We shall now consider each of these two classes in further detail.

Reasoning by Induction
This form of reasoning is based upon the logi-

cal axiom: "What is true of the many is true of the whole." This axiom is based upon man's perception of nature's universal and uniform laws. The process of reasoning in this way may be said to consist of several steps, as follows:

1. Observation. This step consists of the observation, investigation, and examination of a number of particular facts, events, or objects, for the purpose of discovering some general qualities common to many of them. Thus, we might examine a large number of four-footed carnivorous animals and among them we would find a large number possessing a certain set of qualities common to all of that number. The animals possessing these common qualities we would classify under the form of a concept to which we would apply the term "dog." Or, in the same manner we might observe and examine numerous material objects, and thus discover that all of them were attracted to the center of the earth, and a further investigation would discover that all material objects were attracted to each other in a certain way.

2. Hypothesis. The next step in reasoning by induction would be the making of an hypothesis, or general principle assumed as a "possible explanation" of a set or class of facts. Thus, using the previous examples, we would make

an hypothesis that all dogs would act in a certain way under certain circumstances, and that all dogs possessed certain physical and mental characteristics. Of course all dogs were not examined, and could not be examined, but a sufficient number had been examined to justify the making of an hypothesis that all dogs were so and so, and would act so and so. The reasoning was based upon the axiom: "What is true of the many is true of the whole." In the same way, this form of reasoning resulted in the hypothesis known as the Law of Gravitation.

An hypothesis which has been verified by continued observation, experiment, and investigation is advanced in rank and is known as a Theory. Further verification sometimes advances a Theory to the rank of a Law. A writer says of the making of hypothesis: "The forming of an hypothesis requires a suggestive mind, a lively fancy, a philosophic imagination that catches a glimpse of the idea through the form or sees the Law standing behind the fact." Another writer says: "Accepted theories, in most cases, arise only by testing out and rejecting many promising hypothesis and finally settling upon the one which best answers all the requirements and best explains the facts."

3. Testing. The next step in reasoning by induc-

tion is that of testing the hypothesis by deductive reasoning. This is done on the principle of: "If so-and-so is correct, then it follows that thus-and-so is true. If the conclusion agrees with reason and experience, the hypothesis is considered to be reasonable so far as the investigation has proceeded, at least; and, likewise, if the conclusion is found to be inconsistent with reason, or to be a logical absurdity, then the hypothesis is placed under suspicion or may even be utterly rejected. Applying the test to the dog family, the result would be favorable to the hypothesis that "all dogs are so-and-so, and act thus-and-so," if the additional number of dogs examined proved really to possess the assumed general qualities, and to act in the manner assumed in the hypothesis. Likewise, the hypothesis concerning gravitation would be regarded with more favor when it was discovered that the theory met the test of additional observed phenomena.

4. Verification. The final step in reasoning by induction is that of verification resulting from extended and continued observation and testing. A writer says of this: "The greater the number of facts agreeing with the hypothesis, the greater the degree of the 'probability' of the latter. The authorities generally assume an hypothesis to be 'verified' when it accounts for all the facts

which properly are related to it.

Some extremists contend, however, that before an hypothesis may be considered as absolutely verified it must not only account for all the associated facts but that there must also be no other possible hypothesis to account for the same facts. The verification of an hypothesis must be an 'all around one,' and there must be an agreement between the observed facts and the logical conclusions in the case—the hypothesis must fit the facts, and the facts must fit the hypothesis. The facts are like the glass slipper of the Cinderella legend. The several sisters of Cinderella were like imperfect hypotheses, for the slipper did not fit them, nor did they fit the slipper. When Cinderella's foot was found to be the one foot upon which the glass slipper fitted, then the Cinderella hypothesis was considered to be verified—the glass slipper was hers, and the prince claimed his bride." Of two "possible" hypothesis, that one is preferred which best accounts for the greatest number of facts concerning the thing under consideration.

The following quotations from eminent authorities will serve to impress you with the important part played by Reasoning by Induction in our general processes of Thought. A writer says: "The basic principle of inductive reasoning is

'What is true of the many is true of the whole.' This principle is founded upon our faith in the uniformity of Nature. Take away this belief, and all inductive reasoning falls. The basis of induction is thus often stated to be Man's faith in the uniformity of Nature.

"Induction has been compared to a ladder upon which we ascend from facts to laws. This ladder cannot stand unless it has something to rest upon; and this something is our faith in the constancy of Nature's laws."

Another says: "The judgment that 'All men are mortal' was reached by induction. It was observed that all past generations of men had died, and this fact warranted the conclusion that all men living will die. We make the assertion as boldly as if we had seen them all die. The premise that 'All cows chew the cud' was laid down after a certain number of cows had been examined. If we were to see a cow twenty years hence, we should expect to find that she chewed the cud. It was noticed by astronomers that after a certain number of days the earth regularly returned to the same position in its orbit, the sun rose in the same place, and the day was of the same length. Hence, the length of the year and of each succeeding day was determined; and the almanac maker now infers that the same will be true of future years. He tells us that the sun on the first of next December will rise at a given time, though he cannot throw himself into the future to verify the conclusion.

"Every time a man buys a piece of beef, a bushel of potatoes, or a loaf of bread, he is basing his action on inference from induction. He believes that beef, potatoes, or a loaf of bread will prove nutritious food, though he has not actually tested those special edibles before purchasing them. They have hitherto been found to be nutritious on trial, and he argues that the same will prove true of those special instances.

"We instinctively believe in the uniformity of Nature; if we did not, we should not consult our almanacs. If sufficient heat will cause phosphorus to burn today, we conclude that the same result will follow tomorrow, if the circumstances are the same."

Finally, it should be noted that the Major Premise of Reasoning by Deduction (which we shall consider presently)—the main fact assumed to be true in order to reason further by deduction—is nothing more nor less than the Hypothesis, Theory, Law, or Principle discovered in the process of Reasoning by Induction just described and considered by us. Deductive

Reasoning accepts this Major Premise as a fact, making no further inquiry concerning the truth of the same, and then proceeds to draw conclusions from it by certain methods of its own, as we shall presently see.

Reasoning by Deduction

Reasoning by Induction is based upon the axiom: "What is true of the whole, is true of its parts," In the phase of reasoning which we have just considered, i.e. Reasoning by Induction, we discovered a General Law through and by an examination of particular facts. In the present phase of reasoning, i.e. Reasoning by Deduction, we seek to discover particular facts by an application of the aforesaid Law.

An example of this form of reasoning is as follows: Assuming as a general law or principle that "All fish are cold-blooded"; and then making the following statement regarding a living creature placed before us: "This creature is a fish;" we then reach by deductive reasoning the conclusion that: "This creature is cold-blooded." We make this judgment purely by reason, for we have not actually examined that particular fish. If the creature was afterward found not to be cold-blooded, we would be justified in reasoning thusly: "All fish are cold-blooded; this creature is not cold-blooded; therefore, this

281

creature is not a fish."

In the above simple example we have an illustration of the general principles of all Reasoning by Deduction. All of our reasoning of this kind follows the same general rule. We may object that we do not consciously follow such rule, but consciously, or unconsciously, the rule is followed by all persons arriving at conclusions by this form of reasoning. We are not conscious of the several steps of the process, for we have become so accustomed to them from early childhood that they have become almost automatic, or "reflex" with us. As a writer says: "Most persons are surprised when they find out that they have been using logical forms, more or less correctly, without having realized it. A large number even of educated persons have no clear idea of what logic is. Yet, in a certain way, every one must have been a logician since he began to speak."

We shall try to avoid the use of technical logical terms as explanations here. Let us, however, stop a moment to consider just one technical term, namely, "The Syllogism." The Syllogism has been defined as: "An argument expressed in strict logical form, so that its conclusiveness is manifest from the structure of the form alone, without any regard to the meaning of the terms." You may see the truth of the above definition by stating the argument about the fish (previously given) as follows: "All A is Z; Aa is A; therefore, Aa is Z." You will see that the argument is just as sound in this form as in the "fish form." The second "fish" argument may be stated in this form, with equal force and validity: "All A is Z; Aa is not Z; therefore, Aa is not A."

But do not consider that because an argument may proceed to a logical conclusion, that that conclusion must necessarily be true. Remember this always: "If the Major Premise is false, the Conclusion based on it will be false, even though the process of reasoning may be logically correct." For instance, "The Moon is made of green cheese; that object is the Moon; therefore, that object must be a fine dwelling-place for rats and mice."

A Syllogism must have three, and only three, propositions; these propositions are as follows: (1) Major Premise; (2) Minor Premise; and (3) Conclusion. Here is an example of the above: "1. (Major Premise) All fish are cold-blooded; 2. (Minor Promise) This creature is a fish; 3. (Conclusion) Therefore, this creature is cold-blooded."

We shall not enter into a technical exposition of the many rules and principles of correct Reasoning by Deduction—those interested in the subject are referred to some good elementary text-book on logic for a more detailed discussion of the same. Instead, we shall call your attention to a number of the most common Fallacies, or forms of False-Reasoning, so that by observing the false forms you may (by contrast) arrive at an idea of the correct forms. These false forms may thus most usefully be employed as a "terrible example," serving to warn the student away from the course which has led to such results. As an authority has said: "In learning how to do right, it is always desirable to be informed as to the ways in which we are likely to go wrong. In describing to a man the road which he should follow, we ought to tell him not only the turnings which he is to take but also the turnings which he is to avoid. Similarly, it is a useful part of logic which teaches us the ways and turnings by which people most commonly go astray in reasoning."

Fallacies, Sophistry, and Casuistry
A Fallacy is: "An unsound argument, or mode of arguing which, while appearing to be decisive of a question, is in reality not so; or a fallacious statement or proposition in which the error is not readily apparent." Sophistry is a

Fallacy used to deceive others. Sophistry employed to deceive others regarding their moral obligations of rules of conduct is frequently called Casuistry.

Here follows a collection of the more common forms of Fallacy, with a brief description of the particular character of each, and an indication of the particular point of each in which the false-reasoning is hidden.

The Fallacy of "Begging the Question." This particular form of Fallacy consists of one assuming as a proven and accepted fact something which has not been proved, or which, at least, would not be accepted by the other person were it put squarely before him in the form of a plain question. The gist of this form of Fallacy may be said to be in "the unwarranted assumption of a premise, usually the major premise."

A writer gives as an example of this Fallacy through the following argument expressed as a syllogism: "Good institutions should be united; Church and State are good institutions; therefore, Church and State should be united." The above argument may seem quite reasonable and logical at first thought, but a more careful examination will disclose the fact that the Major Premise, viz., "Good institutions should be united," is a mere impudent assumption lacking proof, and not likely to be accepted if presented plainly and considered carefully. It "sounds good" when stated blandly and with conviction (principally because we accept the Minor Premise), but there is no logical warrant for the assumption that because institutions are "good" they should be "united." Question the Major Premise, and the whole chain of reasoning is broken.

Many public men habitually violate the laws of sound reasoning in this way: they boldly assert a fallacious premise, and then proceed to reason or argue logically from it, the result being that their hearers are confused by the apparently logical nature of the whole argument and the soundness of the conclusion, overlooking the important fact that the basic premise itself is unwarranted and unsound.

Such argument and reasoning is rotten at the core. These men proceed on the principle attributed to Aaron Burr, that "Truth is that which is boldly asserted and plausibly maintained." They carry into practice the policy of one of Bulwer's characters, who said: "Whenever you are about to utter something astonishingly false, always begin with: 'It is an acknowledged fact, etc.,' or 'It is admitted by all,' or 'No thinking person denies.' " Bulwer also makes this character say: "Sir Robert Fulmer was a master of this manner of writing. Thus with a solemn face that great man attempted to cheat. He would say: 'It is a truth undeniable that there cannot be any multitude of men whatsoever, either great or small, but that in the same multitude there is one man among them that in nature hath a right to be King of all the rest—as being the next heir of Adam!' "

In all reasoning and argument, therefore, be sure to first be sure to establish the "reasonableness" of the premises, or basic facts. It is true that no reasoning or argument is possible unless we agree to assume as reasonable, or proved, a certain general or particular proposition; but we are always entitled to take the benefit of the doubt in such a case by challenging the reasonableness of the principle or premise seemingly fallaciously advanced to support the subsequent argument of chain of reasoning. Once admit, or allow to pass unchallenged, a fallacious premise, and you may be led by the nose into an intellectual quagmire or morass, where you will sink up to your neck, or perhaps over your head. A fallacious premise is like a rotten foundation of a building—that which is erected thereon may have been carefully built, and be of sound material, but nevertheless, the whole building is unsafe, dangerous, and not fit for habitation.

A writer has given us the following basic rules of sound reasoning and argument: "(1) Clearly define your terms, and insist upon your opponent doing likewise; (2) Establish the correctness, or reasonableness, of your premises, and insist upon the other side doing the same; (3) Then observe the laws of sound reasoning from premise to conclusion."

The reader will be surprised to discover how many popular ideas, beliefs, and general convictions are based upon arguments and reasoning which "beg the question" grossly in stating their Major Premise. The Master Mind refuses to be so misled, and insists upon the premises being at least "reasonable" and not mere bald and impudent assertions and assumptions.

The Fallacy of Reasoning in a Circle. This form of Fallacy consists in assuming as proof of a proposition the very same proposition itself, stated however in another form ("same in substance, different in form"): For example, the following proposition: "This man is a rascal because he is a rogue; he is a rogue because he is a rascal." (There is here, of course, no proof here that the man is either a rascal or a rogue.)

288

This may sound foolish, but many arguments are no sounder, and are based on the same general principles. Here is an "explanation" given under this fallacious principle: "We are able to see through glass, because it is transparent; we know that it is transparent, because we can see through it."

Here are more complex forms: "The Republocratic Party is the right party, because it advocates the right principles; the Republocratic principles are the right principles, because they are advocated by the right party." Or again: "The Church of England is the true Church, because it was established by God; it must have been established by God, because it is the true Church." Or, again "The prophet was inspired; we know that he was inspired because he, himself, so stated, and being inspired he must have spoken only the truth."

As a writer has said: "This particular form of Fallacy is most effective and dangerous when it is employed in long arguments, it being often quite difficult to detect its presence in long discourses in which the two statements of the same thing (in different form) are separated by other words and thoughts."

Irrelevant Conclusion. This Fallacy consists in injecting into the Conclusion something not contained in the Premises. For example: "All men are sinners; John Smith is a man; therefore, John Smith is a horse thief." Many solemn statements made by public men, and others, are really quite as absurd as that just stated, though the absurdity is often lost sight of in the extended statement, and complicated presentation, aided by the solemn, positive air of authority assumed by the speaker. A more plausible form is as follows: "All thieves are liars; John Brown is a liar; therefore, John Brown is a thief." In this last, the statement ignores the fact that while "all thieves are liars," all liars are not necessarily thieves. Remember the old saying: "All biscuits are bread; but all bread is not biscuit."

False Cause. This fallacy consists in assuming a false relation of Cause and Effect between things merely occurring at the same time at the same place; a Coincidence is not necessarily a Cause. There follow typical examples: "The cock crows just before sunrise; therefore, the cock-crow causes the sun to rise." Or, "The Demo-publican administration was accompanied by bad crops; therefore, the Demo-publican Party in power is the cause of bad crops, and therefore should be kept out of power." Or,

"Where civilization is highest, there we find the greatest number of high silk hats; therefore, high silk hats are the cause of high civilization." In the same way, a symptom or a consequence of a condition is often mistaken for the cause of the condition.

Burden of Proof. It is a favorite device of sophistical reasoners to attempt without due warrant to throw the Burden of Proof upon the opponent; particularly when this is employed to establish the truth of the sophist's contention, because the opponent is unable to "prove that it isn't true." The absurdity and fallacious nature of this is more clearly perceived when the proposition is illustrated by a ridiculous example, as for instance: "The moon is made of green cheese; this must be admitted by you to be true, because you cannot prove the contrary." The answer to such a fallacious argument is, of course, the statement that the Burden of Proof rests upon the person making the statement, not on his opponent; and that Proof does not consist in the mere absence of disproof, but rather in the positive evidence advanced to support the proposition advanced. In this connection one recalls the old story about the lawyer in court who produced three men who swore that he saw John Doe strike Richard Roe; whereupon the other side offered to produce a hundred men

to swear that they didn't see him do it—this
sounded well until it was shown that none of
the hundred men were present on the scene of
the fight at all.

Abuse of Opponent. It is no argument, or true
reasoning, to abuse the opponent, or the general
character of those holding contrary opinions.
This is a direct evolution of the ancient argument of beating the opponent over the head
with a club, and then claiming a logical victory.
Likewise it is not a sound argument, nor logical
reasoning, to appeal from the principle under
consideration to the personal practices of the
person advocating the practice. For instance,
a man arguing the advantages of Temperance
may be very intemperate himself; but to point
to his intemperate habits is no proof or argument that the principle of Temperance is incor-
rect. Many a man fails to live up to the principles he teaches to be correct. It may be logically
argued, in the above case, that belief in Temperance does not always cause a man to be temper-
ate; but there is no proof here that the practice
of Temperance is not advisable—in fact, the
man's habits may even be urged as an argument
in favor of Temperance, rather than against it.
The Fallacy is readily detected when one con-
siders that the man may change his habits so
as to square with his belief; and in such case it

cannot be held that a change in the man's habits changes the principle from untruth into truth. A proposition is either true or untrue, regardless of the personal character of the persons advocating or presenting it.

Prejudice. Prejudice is "an unreasonable predilection for, or objection to, anything; especially, an opinion or leaning adverse to anything, without just grounds, or before sufficient knowledge." Prejudice arises from Feeling, not from Reason. Take away from Prejudice the Feeling element therein, and there is little left to it. When we form judgments from Feeling, we frequently perpetrate Fallacy. And, yet, the average person performs the greater part of his decisions, and makes the greatest number of his judgments, in this way—he is ruled by Prejudice rather than by Reason.

A writer says: "Many persons reason from their feelings rather than from their intellect. They seek and advance not true reasons, but excuses. They seek to prove a thing to be true, simply because they want it to be true. The tendency is to see only those facts which agree with our likes, or are in line with our prejudices; and to ignore the other set of facts. Such persons unconsciously assume the mental attitude which may be expressed as follows: 'If the facts do not agree with my pet theories or prejudices, so much the worse for the facts.' "

Another writer says: "Nine times out of ten, to argue with any man on a subject that engages his emotions is to waste breath. His mind is not open to logical persuasion. His emotions first determines his opinion and then prompt his logical faculties to devise plausible excuses for it. There is a thing that psychologists call a 'complex.' It consists of an idea charged with emotion, and it operates as a sort of colored screen in front of the mind. A man whose emotions are deeply engaged on one side of a question may think that he is reasoning about it. But, in fact, he may be incapable of reasoning about it, because whatever impressions his mind receives in that connection come through his complex and take no color. His logical faculties operate only by way of inventing plausible defenses for the judgment his emotions have already formed. It is impossible to change his position in any respect by reasoning, because reason cannot touch his mind until his emotions have dealt with it and made it conform to their color. Whenever you talk to a person with a strong bias on any particular subject, which bias does not coincide with your own bias, talk to him about something else."

Illogical Deduction. There are a number of phases of Fallacy arising from the violation of the technical rules of the Syllogism, which violation results in deduction opposed to the principles of logic. These points are too technical to be considered in detail here, and the reader who wishes to pursue the subject further is referred to some elementary text-book on the subject of Logic.

General Suggestions

The following general suggestions, culled from different writers, will perhaps prove of interest and use to you in your consideration of the general principles of Reasoning.

A writer says: "Most of the work of effective Thinking consists in the observance of a few elementary maxims, as follows: (1) All proof begins with something which cannot be proved, but can only be perceived or accepted, and is called an axiom or first principle; (2) There can be no argument save between those who accept the same first principle; (3) An act can only be judged by defining its object; and (4) Anything can be defended which is not a contradiction in terms. A very slender equipment of such tests would save many people from wasting their time and conscience upon discussions and argument of which they realize neither the origin or the end."

Another writer says: "There is no royal road to the cultivation of the reasoning faculties." There is by the old familiar rule: "Practice, practice, practice." Nevertheless there are certain studies which tend to develop the faculties in question. The study of arithmetic, especially mental arithmetic, tends to develop correct habits of reasoning from one truth to another— from cause to effect. Better still is the study of geometry; and best of all, of course, is the study of logic and the practice of working out its problems and examples. The study of philosophy and psychology also is useful in this way. Many lawyers and teachers have drilled themselves in geometry solely for the purpose of developing their logical reasoning powers."

Another writer says: "So valuable is geometry as a discipline that many lawyers and others review their geometry every year in order to keep the mind drilled to logical habits of thinking. The study of logic will aid in the development of the power of deductive reasoning. It does this, first, by showing the method by which we reason; to see the laws which govern the reasoning process, to analyze the syllogism and see its conformity to the laws of thought, is not only an exercise of reasoning but also gives that knowledge of the process that will be both a stimulus and a guide to thought. No one can trace the principles and processes of thought without receiving thereby an impetus to thought. In the second place, the study of logic is probably even more valuable because it gives practice in deductive thinking. This, perhaps, is its principal value, since the mind reasons instinctively without knowing how it reasons. One can think without the knowledge of the science of thinking, just as one can use language correctly without a knowledge of grammar; yet as the study of grammar improves one's speech, so the study of logic can but improve one's thought."

Another writer says: "We cannot infer anything we please from any premises we please. We must conform to certain definite rules or principles. Any violation of them will be a fallacy. There are two simple rules which should not be violated, viz., (1) The subject-matter in the Conclusion should be of the same general kind as in the Premises; (2) the facts constituting the Premises must be accepted and must not be fictitious."

Another writer says: "When you find yourself fluctuating back and forth between two opinions you might find it helpful to hold an internal debate. State to yourself as strongly as possible the case for the affirmative, and then put as convincingly as possible the case for the negative, holding a refutation if necessary. You may even elaborate this by writing the arguments for both sides in parallel columns. Of course, you should never use an argument which you can see on its face to be fallacious, nor a statement which represents merely a prejudice and nothing more. You should use only such arguments as you think a sincere debater would conscientiously employ. By thus making your reasons articulate you will find that there is really no tenable case at all for one side, and you will seldom fail to reach a definite conclusion."

Again: "The pragmatic method can be applied with profit to nearly all our positive problems. Before starting to solve a question—while deciding, for instance, on the validity of some nice distinction in logic—we should ask ourselves, 'What practical difference will it make if I hold one opinion or another? How will my belief influence my action?' (using the word 'action' in its broadest sense). This may often lead our line of inquiry into more fruitful channels, keep us from making fine but needless distinctions, help us to word our question more relevantly, and lead us to make distinctions where we really need them."

The Master Mind detaches itself from its mental machinery and tools, occasionally and as a matter of exercise, and enters into the full realization of its real existence and real supremacy. Over its mental field it exclaims to itself: "I am the master of all this!" And, in this spirit it imposes its authority upon its tools and machinery, and bids them to perform its work efficiently and intelligently. When Feeling is necessary to stimulate thought and intellectual endeavor, the Master Mind pulls the lever of Feeling and Emotion, and throws its power into the machinery. Likewise, when it perceives that Feeling and Emotion are clogging and "gumming up" the free movement of the intellectual machinery, then the Master Mind reverses the Emotional Lever and decreases its power.

In short, the Ego—the Master Mind, and the Mind Master—takes the central place of power and authority, and manages, controls, and directs the entire mental machinery. The methods which we have indicated and pointed out in this chapter are but suggestions to the Master Mind as to how it may obtain the best, most profitable, and most confident work out of its mental machinery concerned with Thought and Reasoning. But the real direction must come from the Master Mind itself in the form of WILL.

The Intellect is like a good servant, and will listen carefully to, and faithfully obey, the commands issued to it by the Master Mind through the medium of the Will.

In this chapter we have pointed out to the Master Mind just how its intellectual machinery works and operates, and how it may be directed efficiently. But the Master Mind must actually exercise its directing and controlling power itself. The Intellect may be compared to a high-powered automobile. The Master Mind is the driver thereof. These chapters are the "Book of Directions" which the driver studies, and whose principles he applies. But, at the last, the driver must do the real driving, steering, and directing; his hand touches the buttons, and pulls the levers and shuts on and off the Power of the Will to or from certain parts of the machinery. The efficient chauffeur always drives the machine—he never allows the machine to run away with him. The Master Mind should follow the example of the good chauffeur.

Subconscious Mentality

The old psychology held that mind and the ordinary consciousness were practically identical. All mind was supposed to lie in the open field of consciousness, and everything outside of that field was supposed to dwell outside of the realm of mind. Memory was thought to be explained by some vague and non-understandable properties of the brain-cells, by means of which impressions were made upon the brain-matter, and afterward returned to the mind under pressure of the will, or otherwise. This conception was recognized as faulty and unsatisfactory, but it was adopted and held tentatively for a long time simply because nothing more satisfactory presented itself.

But the old idea has now passed into the "scrap heap" of psychology, and is held at the present time only by a few antiquated and stubborn adherents of the old school, whose minds are apparently incapable of acquiring any new impressions, and who desperately try to hold on the shadows of the old, discarded theories, refusing to accept the later and well fortified theories of the modern school of psychology.

The newer conception of psychology holds that a large share of the mental processes of the individual are performed in some fields, or on some planes, of mentality under or above the ordinary plane of consciousness. This idea, once suggested and supported by eminent authorities, has spread rapidly over the thinking world, and at the present time is the accepted teaching of the best schools of psychological thought. In it is found the long sought for explanation of Memory, Imagination, and the so-called Unconscious Cerebration of the older psychologists.

The following statement of the accepted teaching on the subject is reproduced from my work on Memory Training, and is offered here chiefly because of its conciseness:

"Briefly stated the best teaching of today holds that instead of the ordinary consciousness being all there is of mind, it really is but a very small (though highly important) field of the mind's work. The greater part of the mental activities of the individual is performed outside of this narrow field, and only its results are presented to the ordinary consciousness when called for. The ordinary field of consciousness has been well compared to the field of a microscope or telescope, which covers and takes in only that which is presented to it from the great area surrounding it. On the other planes of mind, or other fields of its operations—use which ever term you prefer—are performed great quantities of mental work, classification, analysis, synthesis, adjustment, combination, etc. These subconscious planes or fields of mind may be said to grind, digest, and assimilate the facts impressed upon it through the medium of the senses, or ideas from the conscious field itself. And, moreover, this subconscious plane or field of mind is the great record storehouse of the memory. In it are contained all the records of past impressions, and from it everything that is remembered, recalled, or recollected must come and he re-presented to the conscious mind.

"There is no need of dragging in here the many theories concerning the quality of mind, or the idea that man has two minds. The best thought on the subject is that instead of man having 'two minds,' he really has but one mind, and this one mind has many planes or fields of activity, of which the ordinary consciousness is but one field, and a small one at that. I will go still further, and say that the so-called 'sub-conscious' or 'unconscious' planes of mind are not unconscious, but are really conscious in various degrees of consciousness peculiar to themselves. The term 'sub-conscious' is used simply to indicate that the processes and activities of these particular planes of mind are outside of the field of the ordinary consciousness. When I speak of the passing of impressions, ideas, or records in and out of consciousness, I am not trying to convey the idea of passing these mental images from one mind to another, but rather of passing them in and out of the narrow field of the ordinary consciousness, just as the tiny living creatures in a drop of stagnant water, under a microscope, pass in and out of the field of vision of the apparatus; or as the stars pass in and out of the field of a stationery telescope, as the earth revolves."

The following quotations from eminent authorities in modern psychology will give the reader an idea of the general principle held to be correct by the modern school of that branch of science:

"Mental events imperceptible to consciousness are far more numerous than the others, and of the world which makes up our being we only perceive the highest points—the lighted-up peaks of a continent whose lower levels remain in the shade. Outside a little luminous circle lies a large ring of twilight, and beyond this an indefinite night. But the events of this twilight, and this night, are as real as those within the luminous circle." "Examine closely, and without bias, the ordinary mental operations of daily life, and you will surely discover that consciousness has not one-tenth part of the functions which it's commonly assumed to have. In every conscious state there are at work conscious, subconscious, and infraconscious energies, the last as indispensable as the first."

"It must not be supposed that the mind is at any time conscious of all its materials and powers. At any moment we are not conscious of a thousandth part of what we know. It is well that such is the case; for when we are studying a subject, or an object, we should not want all we know to rush into our minds at the same time. If they did so, our mental confusion would be indescribable. Between the perception and the recall, the treasures of memory are, metaphorically speaking, away from the eye of consciousness. How these facts are preserved, before they are recalled by the call of memory, consciousness can never tell us. An event may not be thought of for fifty years, and then it may suddenly appear in consciousness. As we grow older, the subconscious field increases.

"Where are our images in memory when they are not present in consciousness? The theory is that the full fledged idea is in the mind, but slumbering beneath the stream of consciousness, just as a person is alive when sound asleep, without being aware of the fact. When we are not conscious of an idea, it is believed to disappear just as a diver does beneath the surface of the water; and the one is held to keep its form as intact as the other, during this disappearance."

"Our conscious mind, as compared with the unconscious mind, has been likened to the visible spectrum of the sun's rays, as compared to the invisible part which stretches indefinitely on either side. We know that the chief part of heat comes from the ultra-red rays that show no light; and the main part of the chemical changes in the vegetable world are the results of the ultra-violet rays at the other end of the spectrum, which are equally invisible to the eye, and are recognized only by their potent effects. Indeed, as these visible rays extend indefinitely on both sides of the visible spectrum, so we may say that the mind includes not only the visible or conscious part, and what we have called the sub-conscious, that which lies below the red line, but also the supra-conscious mind that lies at the other end—all those regions of higher soul and spirit life, of which we are at times vaguely conscious, but which always exist, and link us on to eternal verities, on the one side, as surely as the subconscious mind links us to the body on the other."

The processes and activities of the Subconscious Planes of Mentality—at least those of such as have a practical bearing on the subject of the present book—may be classified as follows: (1) Processes of Memory; (2) Processes of Imagination; (3) Processes of Subconscious Thought. Let us consider each of these briefly, in the above order of classification:

The Processes of Memory.
We have considered the general subject of the memory in extensive detail in our previous work entitled "Memory Training," and cannot hope to present more than a brief outline here. The student is referred to our above-mentioned work if he desires to make a thorough study of this branch of the subject. In the following condensed presentation of the subject, however, the reader should find sufficient to set him upon the right track in the Mastery of Memory.

Memory is: "The faculty of the mind by which it retains the knowledge of previous thoughts, impressions, or events." There are several other terms which are usually regarded as being symptoms with that of Memory, but which really have distinctive shades of special meaning. For instance: Memory is the general term indicating the power of retaining and reproducing past impressions or perception; Remembrance is that exercise of the power of Memory by which the representation of past impressions occurs more or less spontaneously, and without conscious effort of will; Recollection is that exercise of the power of Memory in which there is a more or less conscious and active exercise of the will in the direction of calling back, or bringing to the surface, certain impressions which we are vaguely aware of have previously experienced—in such case there is present a general remembrance of the fact and general nature of such previous experience, and the desire and will to bring them to light in further detail. Reminiscence is that exercise of the power of Memory in which there is a blending of resemblance and recollection, and in which there is a conscious representation and re-assembling of a series of previous experiences, but without that close degree of attention to clearness and detail which distinguishes instances of true recollection—this phase of Memory, in fact, may be said to occupy a middle ground between the extremes of recollection and resemblance, respectively.

The processes of Memory may be said to consist of three more or less distinct activities, viz., (1) the securing of records of impressions; (2) the intelligent storing- away of the records of impressions (including the "indexing and cross-indexing" of such records); and (3) the finding and bringing into consciousness such filed-away stored records. This classification is important, for by an understanding of it one may greatly increase his power of Memory. We shall presently consider each of these several processes in detail, but before doing so we wish to offer for your consideration the following interesting description of the part played by the Subconscious Mentality in the processes of Memory, as noted by a writer on the subject. This writer says:

"The work of the subconscious faculties of the mind in the processes of Memory seems to consist in the presentation of plastic mind-stuff to receive thereon the impressions of the senses, of the imagination, and of the ideas evolved by thought.

"We may best understand the working of these faculties of mind if we will but indulge in the fanciful idea of tiny mental workers in charge of the memory records. Of course there are no such entities, but the memory works as if there were; and we may understand its processes by indulging in this fanciful style of presentation of the facts.

"In the first place, let us imagine these tiny workers as having to hand an unfailing support of tiny plastic records upon which to receive the impressions passed on by the report of our senses, our imagination, and our ideas. Each sensation, thought, or idea make an impression on one of these records, varying in depth and clearness according to the degree of attention bestowed upon it. If the sensation, thought, or idea is repeated, the same record receives it and the impression is deepened. The impression may also be deepened by having the workers bring the record into the field of consciousness, and then allowing the imagination to make repeated impressions upon it. But this last practice sometimes works in an unexpected manner, for the imagination may indulge itself in enlarging, and extending its character, and if this be done several times the record will be changed and it will be almost impossible to distinguish the original impression from those added by the imagination. Common experience shows us the truth of this last statement, for who does not know of cases where people have added to a true tale repeatedly told, until at last it become entirely different from the original facts, and yet the teller of the tale imagines that he is telling the exact truth.

"But these little workers have many other tasks

besides that of taking the impressions. They realize that they are continually being called upon to furnish the Ego with these records, in order that it may avail itself of its stored away facts. In order to do this they must have a perfect system of storing and indexing the records, with countless cross-indexes, cross-references, etc. They must arrange each recorded thought, sensation, or idea so that it may be associated with others of its kind, so that when a record is examined it may bring with it its associations in time, space, and classification, that the Ego may be able to think continuously, intelligently, and orderly. What would be the use of remembering a single fact, or idea, if the associated idea or facts were not to be had? Intelligent thought would be impossible under such circumstances. So important is this Law of Association in Memory, that the entire value of Memory depends upon it. Teachers of Memory Culture lay great stress upon this fact.

They teach their students that in cases where they are unable to recall a desired fact or idea, the next best thing is to think of some associated fact, scene, or idea, and lo! once having laid hold upon a link in the chain, it is merely a matter of time before the missing record is found. It is like a great system of cross-indexing. If you cannot remember a thing, find something associated with it, and then run down the index and you will find what you want."

With the above helpful figurative illustration of the "little helpers" in mind, you are now asked to consider the several various steps in the several Processes of Memory, to which we have previously alluded:

(1) Securing Memory Impressions. It is a self-evident fact that in order to remember or recollect an impression previous experienced, the impression must have left some record of its original presence. We cannot hope to bring to light a letter previously received, unless that letter has been placed on record; if it has been destroyed, it cannot be found, and there is no use looking for it. No argument is needed here.

While it is true that psychology holds that every impression experienced in consciousness is recorded somewhere in the Memory, it is likewise true that most impressions received by us are so shallow and so indistinct that the record thereof scarcely exists, and could not well be clearly reproduced even if found. Let us use the illustration of the wax phonographic cylinder, in our consideration of the subject of the records of Memory. The impressions received on the wax cylinder of Memory must be clearly registered, else we obtain only a faint and blurred presentation when we place the record on the phonographic machine for reproduction.

And here is an important point: The degree of clearness of the memory impression depends upon the degree of Attention which we have given to the original impression. Adhering to our figure of the phonograph, we may say that Attention is the recording needle which makes the record on the wax cylinder of Memory. If the needle-point of Attention is dulled, or encrusted with wax, then there is no clear record—and consequently no possibility of a clear reproduction. If, on the other hand, the needle point of Attention is sharp and clean, then we have a clean, clear, deep record—and consequently a clear, strong reproduction at a later time.

Most persons complaining of a "poor memory" are really suffering from poor Attention. Their first step in Memory Culture should be that of cleaning and sharpening the needle-point of Attention. This may be done by practicing the exercises in Attention previously given in this book, and by following the rules concerning the development of Attention and Concentration given therein.

(2) Storing Away Memory Records. After obtaining a good, clean, clear record on the wax cylinder of the Memory phonograph, the next step is that of filing away and storing away such record in such a way that it may easily be found. It is true that Nature has done much for us in this way, in the direction of furnishing us with subconscious helpers who do the best they can for us. But in our complex modern life we pour into the subconscious storehouse of Memory such a heterogeneous mass and mixture of records that it is no wonder that the powers of the subconscious filing clerks are overtaxed. We can do much to help them, if we will but take the trouble. The process of intelligent storing away and filing of Memory records is greatly aided by an understanding of a very important principle of law of Memory, i.e., the principle of Mental Association. This principle, briefly stated, is this: that every mental impression, sensation, thought, or complex derivatives of these, is bound by associative links to other mental impressions. These associate links are practically "cross-indexes" in the filing-room of Memory. The more cross-index references that an impression or idea has in the filing-room, the more easily it is located, and the more quickly is it recollected. The remembrance of an associated idea, thought, or sensation, will result in a quick and sure recollection of every other men-

tal impression associated with, or connected with it. If you have ever consulted a cross-indexed encyclopedia, or card index system having cross-indexes, you will appreciate the value of this illustration.

Many a time have you failed to recollect a desired impression or idea. You gave it up in despair, and then after a greater or less space of time out popped the forgotten thing into your field of consciousness. "What happened to cause this? Simply this: the subconscious faculties hunted around until they found a "cross-index" of the thing sought for—that is to say, they found a record or some other thing connected or associated with the original impression in some way or other, probably by association is space, time, or resemblance—and that started up a process of intelligent further search that ended in success. If the thing had been better cross-indexed by you, you could have recalled it in a moment or two, as you always do in such cases. The Rule of Association is: Associate each thing that you wish to remember, with as many other things as possible which will be likely to suggest the thing to you. Use natural (not artificial) associative links in this way. You know from experience that if you recall or remember the circumstances of the occurrence of a thing—the surrounding scene, incidents, etc.—

then you find it comparatively easy to recall to consciousness the thing itself.

Do not waste your money or your time in purchasing or studying artificial Memory System embodying methods of artificial association which are harder to remember and recall than the thing itself that you wish to recall. Instead, when you need it, you should link and associate that particular thing to and with as many other suggestive things as possible. Attach to it this memory of the circumstances under which you first heard the thing the people present; the scene; what led up to the thing, and what followed it; and what it reminded you of, and so on, and so on. Not only will this help you to easily recall the thing itself, but it will also develop your general memory, and general fund of knowledge.

(3) Recollection. The final active process of Memory is that of recollection, bringing to light, in short finding the stored away records of Memory and bringing them into the field of consciousness—finding them and placing them into the phonograph for reproduction, so to speak. Providing that you have (a) originally obtained good, clear records; and (b) filed them away properly and intelligently; there then remains simply (c) the effort of desire or will

to bring them to light and consciousness—then to place them once more on the mental phonograph so as to hear them reproduced for you.

Recollection, however, like every other mental or physical activity, depends largely for its efficiency upon Exercise. Therefore, if you will practice a few simple exercises in "recollection" every day, you will find that your "Memory" will rapidly and greatly improve. Most persons take Recollection for granted, and use it only when they need it very much. That is as foolish as to expect that your arm-muscles will be able to perform occasional strenuous tasks without you having previously given them exercise and use. Training, mental and physical, means simply Intelligent Exercise. And there is but one fundamental rule of Exercise, and that is, simply, DO IT!

Once in a while, when you have a little spare time after work hours, sit down and try to recall the occurrences and happenings of the day. You will find that by a little practice you will be able to recall far more of these happenings than you will be able to do at the first trial. Then try to make a mental synopsis of the happenings of the past week, at the end thereof. This sounds easy, but it really is difficult; but you will make wonderful progress if you will persevere. It is related of an eminent American statesman of the last century, that by this simple practice (enlarged upon and varied from time to time) he cured himself of a notoriously "poor Memory," and in its place developed an extraordinarily efficient Memory in all of its phases.

If you will picture to yourself the developing and evolving efficiency of a new filing- clerk in the great Memory of storehouse of records, you will get the right idea. You know very well if you were to be given such a task you would develop efficiency each and every day of your employment, until at last you would be regarded as a "wonder" or a "wizard" at this particular work, do you not? You know that in due time, by reason of practice and experience, you would be able to go directly to the proper file, and then pull out the proper record—just as experienced and practiced filing-clerks do every one of their working days. Then, knowing this, there is no reason for your remaining a "poor recollector." Here is the method—use it!

The Processes of Imagination
Imagination, the second class of the processes of the Subconscious Mentality, very closely resembles its brother, the Memory, but there is an important distinction between the two, as follows: Memory reproduces only the origi-

nal impressions placed within its realm, while Imagination reproduces the recorded impressions of Memory, not in their original condition, but in new groupings, arrangements, and forms.

Memory is the storehouse of impressions, but Imagination is the artist working with these stored up impressions, and making new and wonderful things with the same. Imagination takes these stored-away impressions, and creates new forms of things from them, but always uses the materials it finds in the Memory storehouse—it makes new combinations, new arrangements, new forms, but it never makes new materials.

Some persons think that there are no limits to the power of the Imagination—but this is wrong. There are practically no limits to the new arrangements and new combinations possible to Imagination; but this is about the limit of its powers. For, always, under the manifold and diverse forms of the creations of Imagination there will always be found the "stuff" or "material" which it has obtained from the storehouse of Memory, and which Memory has obtained through Sensation and Perception as we have seen in preceding portions of this book. Imagination, like Memory, has only the "raw materials" of Perception to work with, to build with, and to fashion into new forms, and shapes, and combinations.

You may doubt this. You may say that you can imagine an elephant with the wings of an eagle, the tail of an alligator, the horns of a bull-moose, and the legs of a giraffe— the kind of creature, in fact, that some persons actually do imagine (in dreams, after partaking too freely of the Welsh Rarebit, or the cold Mince Pie). You say, "I have imagined these things, very clearly and distinctly—but I certainly have never seen such a creature, for such does not exist!" But wait a moment, good critic. You have never actually perceived such a creature, of course; but you have perceived (either in real life or in pictured form) each and every one of the characteristics of this impossible animal! You have seen an elephant, an eagle, an alligator, a bull-moose, and a giraffe—and you have abstracted from each of these animals certain characteristics, and then have built up these several characteristics into a new creature which is a product of your imagination. But you haven't created a single new material or part—you have simply re-combined and re-arranged these original perceptions, that's all! And that is all that you, or anyone else, ever has done, or ever can do, by the processes of Imagination.

Imagination is subject to misuse as well as use—in fact, the word is frequently employed to indicate the misuse of it, in the form of idle day dreams and vain fanciful flights of the imagination. This misuse arises from the involuntary exercise of the Imagination—allowing this subconscious faculty to indulge in purposeless and useless activity. This is like mere day-dreaming, and is a habit which often obtains quite a hold over persons if too freely indulged in, and often leading them away from the actualities of life. It is a mild form of mental intoxication, the effects are undesirable, for they often manifest in a weakening of the will, and rendering infirm the voluntary purpositive faculties of the mind.

The most harmful effects of this idle exercise of the imagination is that it usurps the place rightfully belonging to action. It is so much easier and so much more pleasant to dream of accomplishments, than to attempt to make them come true in actual life The habitual day-dreamer gradually loses the desire to participate in the activities of life, and slowly sinks into a mere passive existence, doing as little actual work as possible, and always longing for his hours of dream-life as the morphine victim longs for his drug, or the liquor victim for his glass.

The best modern psychology recognizes this danger of the misuse of the Imagination, and lays great stress upon the necessity of transmuting the energies of the Imagination into the images of things connected with the life work of the individual, character- building, self-mastery, and general creative work along the lines of the Constructive Imagination. Modern psychology holds that the positive use of the Imagination along creative and constructive lines is worthy of cultivation and development by scientific methods, for the reason that by its intelligent and purpositive application it leads to all progress and advancement, attainment and realization. Creative and constructive imagination furnishes the pattern, design, or mold of future action or material manifestation. The imagination is the architect of deeds, actions and accomplishments. A well-known American woman once made the remark that she prayed that her sons might be given the active power of creative and constructive Imagination— and her wish was a wise one, for from that power are derived the plans of future accomplishment.

A leading scientist once said: "Physical investigation, more than anything besides, helps to teach us the actual value and right use of the Imagination—of that wondrous faculty, which, when left to ramble uncontrolled, leads us

astray in a wilderness of perplexities and errors, a land of mists and shadows, but, which,
properly controlled by experience and reflection, becomes the noblest attribute of man,
the source of poetic genius, the instrument of
discovery in science, without the aid of which
Newton would never have invented fluxions nor
Davy have decomposed the earths and alkalis,
nor would Columbus have found another continent." Another great scientist has said: "We are
gifted with the power of imagination, and by
this power we can lighten the darkness which
surrounds the world of our senses. There are
some, even in science, who regard Imagination
as a faculty to be feared and avoided rather than
employed. They have observed its action in
weak vessels, and are unduly impressed by its
disasters. But they might with equal truth point
to exploded boilers as an argument against
the use of steam. Bounded and conditioned by
co-operant reason, Imagination becomes the
mightiest instrument of the physical discoverer.
Newton's passage from a falling apple to a falling moon was, at the outset, a leap of the Imagination."

In this constructive and creative work of the
Imagination we have but another example of
what has been so positively insisted upon, and
repeated, in the foregoing chapters of this book,

namely, the principle of the Ego using its instruments of expression, instead of allowing the later to use the Ego. The Ego uses its imaginative faculties along creative and constructive lines, instead of allowing them to run away with the chariot of the Ego. It is the positive use of the faculties, instead of the negative. It is another illustration of the power of the Master Mind in its work of the Mastery of Mind.

Here follow a few carefully selected rules for the cultivation of the right habits of using the Imagination effectively and efficiently. It will be worth your while to carefully acquaint yourself with the same.

The Supply of Material. Before the Imagination can build, construct, and create, it must be supplied with the proper materials. The materials with which the Imagination works is to be had only in the subconscious storehouse of Memory. Therefore, the Memory must be supplied with a stock of information concerning the particular subject or object which the Imagination is to develop by means of its creative power. And the impressions stored away in this manner should be clear, distinct, and strong.

Develop by Exercise. The Imagination should be developed, cultivated, and strengthened by voluntary and directed exercise and use. Acquire the habit of mapping out the work you have to do in advance, and allowing the creative Imagination to fill in the details of the map after you have made the general outlines. Turn your attention upon the tasks before, and you will find that, providing you have the strong desire for improvement well kindled, the Imagination will set to work suggesting improvements.

Avoid Idle Day-Dreaming. Avoid the habit of idle day-dreaming, for such only dissipates and wastes the energies of the Imagination. Instead, strive to acquire the habit of the purposeful, voluntary use of the Imagination.

Hold to the Central Idea. In the work of Constructive Imagination, always hold firmly to the central idea and central purpose of your thought. Build up, tear down, alter and change the details as much as you see fit, but always with the idea of improving and creating—but never allow yourself to be sidetracked. Let the central idea and its purpose be the skeleton framework upon which you build your structure.

Discard Useless Material. Acquire the habit of discarding all ideas and mental images that are not conducive to your creative work. Hold your mind "one pointed" while engaged in your imaginative work. Subject all your ideas and mental images to the test: "Is this conducive to the task in view? Does this tend to efficiency?" Hold fast to the Positives, and reject the Negatives.

See the Result as You Desire It to Be. Always hold before your mental eye the picture of yourself accomplishing the thing you have set out to do, and also the picture of the result taking on the proper form and power.

The following quotations from eminent authorities will serve to illustrate the principles embodied in the above rules, and will probably give additional inspiration to the reader who wishes to effectively and efficiently use his faculties of Imagination. By viewing the subject from the different angles of vision of these several authorities, you will get a wider and fuller vision of it than from the ideas of any one writer.

"In this age there is no mental power that stands more in need of cultivation than the Imagination. So practical are its results that a man without it cannot possibly be a good plumber. He must image short cuts for placing his pipe. The image of the direction to take to elude an obstacle must precede the actual laying of the pipe. If he fixes it before traversing the way with his Imagination, he frequently gets into trouble and has to tear down his work. Someone has said that the more imagination a blacksmith has, the better will he shoe a horse. Every time he strikes the red-hot iron, he makes it approximate to the image in his mind. Nor is that image a literal copy of the horse's foot. If there is a depression in that, the Imagination must build out a corresponding elevation in the image, and the blows must make the iron fit the image."

"It is certain that in order to execute consciously a voluntary act we must have in the mind a conception of the aim and purpose of the act." "It is as serving to guide and direct our various activities that mental images derive their chief value and importance. In anything that we purpose or intend to do, we must first of all have an idea or image of it in the mind, and the more clear and correct the image, the more accurately and efficiently will the purpose be carried out. We cannot exert an act of volition without having in mind an idea or image of what we will to effect."

"By aiming at a new construction, we must clearly conceive what is aimed at. Where we have a very distinct and intelligible model before us, we are in a fair way to succeed; in proportion as the ideal is dim and wavering we stagger and miscarry."

"When one is engaged in seeking for a thing, if he keep the image of it clearly before the mind he will be likely to find it, and that too, probably where it would otherwise have escaped his notice."

"No one ever found the walking fern who did not have the walking fern in his mind. A person whose eye is full of Indian relics picks them up in every field he walks through. They are quickly recognized because the eye has been commissioned to find them."

So, here too, we find that the Imagination, instead of doing as it likes, when it likes, and how it likes, as many suppose it must be allowed to do, is really as readily amenable to the control, direction, and mastery of the Ego as is any other of the mental processes. The Master Mind is the Master of Imagination, as it is the Master of the rest of the Mental Realm.

The Processes of Subconscious Thought.
The third of the great classes of processes of the Subconscious Mentality is that which be called that of Subconscious Thought. While most persons accept readily the fact of the subconscious

nature of the processes of Memory and Imagination, respectively, they are somewhat skeptical at first concerning the statement that the mind performs a large portion of its thought-processes on those planes of mentality below the plane of the ordinary consciousness.

The subconscious processes of thought are well illustrated by the following statements of eminent authorities:

"At least ninety percent, of our mental life is subconscious, if you will analyze your mental operation you will find that conscious thinking is never a continuous line of consciousness, but a series of conscious data with great intervals of subconsciousness. We sit and try to solve a problem, and fail. Suddenly an idea dawns that leads to a solution of the problem. The subconscious processes were at work."

"Carpenter calls attention to the common experience of subconscious meditation, and illustrates it by the experience of a friend who stated that at one time he had laboriously sought for the solution of a difficult problem, but without success. Then suddenly the solution flashed across his mind, and so complete was the answer, and so unexpected was its appearance, that he trembled as if in the presence of another being who had communicated a secret to him."

"A close attention to our internal operations, along with induction, gives us this result, that we exercise ratiocination of which we have no consciousness, and generally it furnishes us with this marvelous law, that every operation whatsoever of our minds is unknown to us until a second operation reveals it to us."

"The unconscious logical processes are carried out with a certainty and regularity which would be impossible where there exists the possibility of error. Our mind is so happily designed that it prepares for us the most important foundations of cognition, while we have not the slightest apprehension of the modus operandi. This unconscious mentality, like a benevolent stranger, works and makes provision for our benefit, pouring only the mature fruits into, our laps."

"It is inexplicable how premises which lie below consciousness can sustain conclusions in consciousness; how the mind can wittingly take up a mental movement at an advanced stage, having missed its primary steps."

"It is surprising how uncomfortable a person may be made by the obscure idea of something which he ought to have said or done, and which he cannot for the life of him remember. There is an effort of the lost idea to get into consciousness, which is relieved directly the idea bursts into consciousness."

"There are thoughts that never emerge into consciousness, which yet make their influence felt among the perceptive currents, just as the unseen planets sway the movements of the known ones. I was told of a business man in Boston who had given up thinking of an important question as too much for him. But he continued so uneasy in his brain that he feared that he was threatened with palsy. After some hours the natural solution of the question came to him, worked out, it is believed, in that troubled interval."

"We are constantly aware that feelings emerge unsolicited by any previous mental state, directly from the dark womb of unconsciousness. Indeed all our most vivid feelings are thus derived. Suddenly a new irrelevant, unwilled, and unlocked for presence intrudes itself into consciousness. Some inscrutable power causes it to rise and enter the mental presence as a sensorial constituent. If this vivid dependence on unconscious forces has to be conjectured with the most vivid mental occurrences, how much more such a sustaining foundation must be postulated for those faint revivals of previous sensations that so largely assist us in making up our complex mental presence."

"It has often happened to me to have accumulated a store of facts, but to have been able to proceed no further. Then, after an interval of time, I have found the obscurity and confusion to have cleared away, the facts to have settled in their right places, though I have not been sensible of having made any effort for that purpose."

"After days, weeks, or months we often find to our great astonishment that the old opinions we had up to that moment have been entirely rearranged, and that new ones have already become lodged there. This unconscious mental process of digestion and assimilation I have several times experienced in my own case."

"The mind receives from experience certain data, and elaborates them unconsciously by laws peculiar to itself, and the result merges into consciousness."

"Berthelot, the great French chemist, and founder of Synthetic Chemistry, told his intimates that the experiments which led to many of his wonderful discoveries were not the result of carefully followed trains of thought, or of pure reasoning processes, but, on the contrary, they 'came of themselves, so to speak,' as if from the clear sky above."

"At times I have had the feeling of the uselessness of all voluntary effort, and also that the matter was working itself clear in my mind. It has many times seemed to me that I was really a passive instrument in the hands of a person not myself. In view of having to wait for the results of these unconscious processes, I have proved the value of getting together material in advance, and then leaving the mass to digest itself till I am ready to write about it. I delayed for a month the writing of my book, 'System of Psychology,' but continued reading the authorities. I would not try to think about the book. I would watch with interest the people passing the windows. One evening when reading the paper the substance of the missing part of the book flashed upon my mind, and I began to write. This is only a sample of many such experiences."

"My Brownies! God bless them! who do one-half of my work for me when I am fast asleep, and in all human likelihood do the rest for me as well when I am wide awake and foolishly suppose that I do it for myself. I had long been wanting to write a book on man's double being.

For two days I went about racking my brains for a plot of any sort, and on the second night I dreamt the scene in Dr. Jekyll and Mr. Hyde at the window; and a scene, afterward split in two, in which Hyde, pursued, took the powder and underwent the change in the presence of his pursuer. In Otalla, the Count, the mother, Otalla's chamber, the meeting on the stairs, the broken window, were all given me in bulk and details, as I have tried to write them."

Many pages could be filled with similar testimony to the reality of the processes of Subconscious Thought, to which has been given the names "automatic thinking," "unconscious rumination," or even the picturesque term "the helpful Brownies" of Stevenson; but the principle has been clearly illustrated in the above quotations, and further testimony would only be in the nature of repetition. The facts are admitted by all advanced modern psychologists, and many eminent persons have testified as to the manifestation of similar phenomena in their own experience. Many persons have acquired special efficiency in directing their subconscious faculties to perform similar work for them.

Perhaps the most concise and practical directions for manifesting this form of mental process is the following, quoted from an American writer who has made a special study of the subject. This authority says:

"In the Inner Consciousness of each of us there are forces which act much the same as would countless tiny mental brownies or helpers who are anxious and willing to assist us in our mental work, if we will but have confidence and trust in them. This is a psychological truth expressed in the terms of the old fairy tales. The process of calling into service these Inner Consciousness helpers is similar to that by which we constantly employ to recall some forgotten fact or name. We find that we cannot recollect some desired fact, date, or name, and instead of racking our brains with an increased effort, we (if we have learned the secret) pass on the matter to the Inner Consciousness with a silent command, 'Recollect this name for me,' and then go on with our ordinary work. After a few minutes—or it may be hours—all of a sudden, pop! will come the missing name of fact before us—flashed from the planes of the Inner Consciousness, by the help of the kindly workers or 'brownies' of those planes. The experience is so common that we have ceased to wonder at it, and yet it is a wonderful manifestation of the Inner Consciousness workings of the mind. Stop and think a moment, and you will see that the missing word does not present itself accidentally, or 'just because.' There are mental processes at work for your benefit, and when they have worked out the problem for you they gleefully push it up from their plane on to the plane of the outer consciousness where you may use it.

"We know of no better way of illustrating the matter than by this fanciful figure of the 'mental brownies,' in connection with the illustration of the 'subconscious storehouse.' If you would learn to take advantage of the work of these Subconscious Brownies, we advise you to form a mental picture of the Subconscious Storehouse in which is stored all sorts of knowledge that you have placed there during your lifetime, as well as the impressions that you have acquired by race inheritance—racial memory, in fact. The information stored away has often been placed in the storage rooms without any regard for systematic storing, or arrangement, and when you wish to find something that has been stored away there a long time ago, the exact place being forgotten, you are compelled to call to your assistance the little brownies of the mind, which perform faithfully your mental command, 'Recollect this for me!' These brownies are the same little chaps that you charge with the task of waking you at four o'clock tomorrow morning when you wish to catch an early train—and they obey you well in this work of the mental alarm-clock. These same little chaps will also flash into your consciousness the report, 'I have an engagement at two o'clock with Jones'—when looking at your watch you will see that it is just a quarter before the hour of two, the time of your engagement.

"Well then, if you will examine carefully into a subject which you wish to master, and will pass along the results of your observations to these Subconscious Brownies, you will find that they will work the raw materials of thought into shape for you in a comparatively short time. They will arrange, analyze, systematize, collate, and arrange in consecutive order the various details of information which you have passed on to them, and will add thereto the various articles of similar information that they will find stored away in the various recesses of your memory. In this way they will group together various scattered bits of knowledge that you have forgotten. And, right here, let us say to you that you never absolutely forget anything that you have placed in your mind. You may be unable to recollect certain things, but they are not lost— sometime later some associative connection will be made with some other fact, and lo! the missing idea will be found fitted nicely into its place in the larger idea—the work of our little brownies. Read the examples given of the eminent persons who have had experiences of this kind. These; experiences can be reproduced by you when you have acquired the 'knack of it.'

Remember Thompson's statement: 'In view of having to wait for the results of these unconscious processes, I have proved the habit of getting together material in advance, and then leaving the mass to digest itself until I am ready to write about it.' This subconscious 'digestion' is really the work of our little mental brownies.

"There are many ways of setting the brownies to work. Nearly everyone has had some experience, more or less, in the matter, although often it is produced almost unconsciously, and without purpose and intent. Perhaps the best way for the average person—or rather the majority of persons—to get the desired results is for one to get as clear an idea of what one really wants to know—as clear an idea or mental image of the question you wish answered. Then after rolling it around in your mind— mentally chewing it, as it were—giving it a high degree of voluntary attention, you can pass it on to your Subconscious Mentality with the mental command: 'Attend to this for me—work out the answer!'

or some similar order. This command may be given silently, or else spoken aloud—either will do. Speak to the Subconscious Mentality—or its little workers—just as you would speak to persons in your employ, kindly but firmly. Talk to the little workers, and firmly command them to do your work. And then forget all about the matter—throw it off your conscious mind, and attend to your other tasks. Then in due time will come your answer—flashed into your consciousness—perhaps not until the very minute that you must decide upon the matter, or need the information. You may give your brownies orders to report at such and such a time—just as you do when you tell them to awaken you at a certain time in the morning so as to catch the early train, or just as they remind you of the hour of your appointment, if you have them well trained."

The above instruction, though conveyed in a fanciful style in order to catch the attention and to be easily remembered, really contains the essence and substance of the most approved methods of making use of the faculties of the subconscious mentality in the process of Subconscious Thought. The reader should carefully study this method, and begin to practice it as he wishes to make use of this wonderful power of the mind. He will find that after a little practice his mental powers will be enormously increased, and his general efficiency likewise added to.

Here, as elsewhere, we have the fact set forth that the Ego is the Master Mind, ruling, controlling, directing and managing his subjects, the mental faculties. The Ego—the Master Mind—has a large realm over which to rule, and many subjects to govern; but it has the power to govern them properly and efficiently, providing that it will awaken to its own reality and power, and will grasp firmly the scepter of authority which rightfully belongs to it, but which it may have allowed to drop from its relaxed fingers while it slept.

The Mastery of Will

There is probably no phase of mental activity which is more difficult to define than that called the Will. All of us know quite well what is meant by "the will," but when we attempt to express the knowledge in formal words we find it most difficult. When we refer to the dictionaries for assistance, we are but little better off, for they generally hold fast to the old philosophical conception of Will as (1) the desire or inclination to act in a certain way, or (2) the power of choice exercised by the mind, by which it decides which of several courses of action to follow. The third, and according to the modern view the most important phase of will, namely, that of the act of voluntary effort and actions, is passed over in most cases as being merely incidental.

The modern conception of the Will is that of mental states concerned with action, the other phases being regarded as subordinate to this. As a popular psychologist has well stated: "Will concerns itself with action. The student must keep that fact before him, no matter how complex the process seems. We are never without the activity of the will, in the broadest sense of that term.

The Will may be said to present three general phases of itself for our consideration, namely: (1) The phase in which Desire is being transformed into Will; (2) the phase in which there is the process of Deliberation concerning the respective values of several desires, or several courses of action represented by their respective ideas or mental images; this phase of Deliberation begins with conflicting motives, and ends with a Decision or Choice; (3) the phase of action resulting from the Decision or Choice. The following somewhat fuller statement of each of these phases will aid the reader in perceiving the special characteristics of each.

1. Desire-Will. All activities of the Will may be said to have been preceded by Desire. One may Desire without actually setting the Will into operation, but one can scarcely be thought of as Willing without having first experienced the Desire to Will (it being, of course, understood that such Desire may have manifested subconsciously rather than in the conscious field). It is almost impossible to conceive of one willing to do a thing unless from the motive of Desire, either in the form of "wanting to" on the one hand, or that of fear on the other hand. At the last, as at the first, Will is seen to be the active expression of some form of Desire.

A writer says: "Desire is aroused by feelings or emotions rising from the subconscious planes of the mind, and seeking expression and manifestation. In some cases the feeling or desire first manifests in a vague unrest caused by subconscious promptings and excitement. Then the imagination pictures the object of the feeling, or certain memory images of it, and the desire thus rises to the plane of consciousness. The entrance of the desiring feeling into consciousness is accompanied by that particular tension which marks the second phase of desire. This tension, when sufficiently strong, passes into the third phase of desire, or that in which desire blends into will-action. Desire in this stage makes a demand upon will for expression and action. From mere feeling, and tension of feeling, it becomes a call to action. But before expression and action are given to it, the second phase of will must manifest at least for a moment; this second phase is known as deliberation, or the weighing and balancing of desires."

2. Deliberative Will. In this second phase of Will activity, there is a balancing and weighing of desires, or at least a weighing and balancing of several courses of action in order to determine their values as a channel of expression of the strongest desires.

Sometimes there is present a dominant desire that presses aside all other desires, and asserts its strength and power; in such a case the deliberation is simply that of determining the best possible channel of expression of that desire. But, as a rule, there is first a conflict of desires, which results either in the victory of the strongest desire present at that moment, or else an average struck between several strong desires then present.

In the case of an uncultured person, the struggle is based upon the most primitive and elemental factors of feeling, but with the development of intellect new factors manifest themselves and exert their influence. Also, the more complex the emotional development of the individual, the more intense and complicated becomes the process of choice. Reference to the foregoing chapters in which the subject of the nature of Desire is considered, will throw additional light on this subject. In the case of individuals of higher emotional and intellectual culture, it will be found that the desires concerning the welfare of other persons in whom the individual has a keen interest and for whom he has a great affection will often prove stronger than the more personal feelings. Likewise, in such an individual the prospect of a future greater benefit will often outweigh a lesser though immediate benefit.

As a writer says: "The judgment and action of an intelligent man, as a rule, are far different from those of an unintelligent one; and a man of culture tends toward different action than that of an uncultured one; and, likewise, the man of broad sympathies and high ideals acts in a different way from one of the opposite type. But the principle is always the same—the feelings manifest in desire, the greatest ultimate satisfaction apparent at the moment is sought, and the strongest set of desires wins the day."

Finally, the balance is struck, and the decision or choice is made, and the individual "makes up his mind" to act in accordance therewith. And, in the ordinary course, the process of Will then passes on to the next phase, i.e., the phase of Action.

3. Action-Will. The older psychologists usually passed at once from the phase of Will called "Deliberation," into that phase called "Action." But the newer school is more discriminating, and insists that there is an intermediate stage between the two said phases—a stage in which, though decision and choice be made, and though action may be determined upon, still there is a holding-back from actual action.

A typical illustration of this intermediate stage is the familiar experience of rising in the morning. We may resolve to get up, because we see the need of doing so and the penalty for not doing so; then we firmly "make up our mind" to rise, but for some reason we linger a little longer, and our resolve does not take form in action. Finally, for some reason, we suddenly seem to appreciate the need of immediate action, and then the spring of the will is released, and we throw off the covers and step out of the bed.

A well-known psychologist says: "From a subjective point of view, decision may end the matter, but in a practical world decision is of little account unless it is followed by action. The road to hell is said to be paved with good intentions, or decisions. A good decision never moved a person an inch heavenward. For a completed act of will, there must be action along the line of the decision. Many a decision has not raised the motor centers to action, nor quickened the attention, for any length of time. There are persons who can frame a dozen decisions in the course of a morning, and never carry out one of them. Sitting in a comfortable chair, it may take one but a very short time to form a decision that will require months of hard work. Deciding in this way is very different from laboring wearily to carry the decision into effect. The decider does not generally realize the amount of effort involved when he airily declares his intention of performing a certain action.

"Some persons can never seem to understand that resolving to do a thing is not the same as doing it. Such are utterly worthless in this world of action. They talk; they feel; they do anything but act. They appear to derive almost as much comfort from resolving to answer a letter, which should have been answered two months before, as they would from actually writing the reply. There may be desire, deliberation, and decision; but if these do not result in action along the indicated line, the process of will is practically incomplete."

Training the Will
Just as the Master Mind may train the faculties of Thought, and the faculties of Feeling and Emotion, so may it train, control, direct, and master the faculties of the Will. And this last is perhaps the most important of all the various forms of mastery manifested by the Ego, or Master Mind, because the Will is the instrument which the Ego applies to control the other mental faculties—and control of the Will is control of the entire situation.

It should be mentioned here, however, that if the student has put into practice the various forms of the control of the other mental faculties, the Will itself will be found to have gained strength and power from such use and exercise. Particularly is this so where the Attention has been mastered and controlled, for the Attention is the principal weapon of the Will—the one by which it imposes its authority upon the other faculties.

The following Rules for Will-Training will furnish the student with a simple, practical method or system of training and cultivating the Will. It consists of the application of a few elemental principles, which may be afterward elaborated, added-to, and developed into a much more imposing structure of method and system.

The Rules of Will Development
1. Finding the Center of Power. This rule consists of bidding the student to find the center of his mental being—the place where dwells the Ego, the Master of Mind, the "I." This consists not alone of him merely assenting to the presence of the Ego on the part of the intellect, but rather of the conscious feeling of the presence, reality and power of the "I," in the center of the mental field, where it masters, directs, controls,

and manages the feelings, emotions, thought processes, objects of attention and desire, and finally of the activities of the will.

The Ego must learn to turn its attention inward upon itself, and to be conscious of its own presence and existence. It must inwardly cognize itself as the "I"—an actual living entity or being. To do this fully, the Ego must for the moment separate itself from the various instruments and faculties belonging to it—it must see and feel itself simply as the pure Ego—the "I AM!" It may take some time and practice for one to attain this particular stage of self-consciousness, but progress will be made from the beginning, and each step of the path will be repaid with actual results. Each time you control or direct the mind, say to yourself "I, the Ego, the Master Mind, am doing this"—and you will be made conscious of a dawning realization of the Ego which is Yourself—your Real Self.

2. Exert Your Will Power. Exert Your Will Power by practicing the control over the several mental and emotional faculties. Will to think; Will to feel; Will to act. For instance: you may feel a desire to do, or not to do a certain thing— here is your chance to prove your Will Power. Deliberately determine that you shall and will desire and feel the exact opposite of your pres-

ent desire, and then proceed to manifest in action that idea and determination. You will find that the original desire or feeling will struggle and rebel—it will fight hard for life and power—but you must oppose it to the deadly cold steel of your will, as directed by the Master Mind, or Ego. Persevere, and yield not an inch—assert your mastery of your own mental domain. Ask no quarter, and give none; and as sure as tomorrow's sun will rise, so surely will your will triumph, for the Will is positive to the other mental states, when it is properly applied and persistently exerted.

3. Consider Your Actions. Cultivate the faculty of careful deliberation and intelligent determination. In short, look before you leap. Test your feelings, emotions, impulses, and desires by the light of your intellect. Test every desire and impulse by the Touchstone of Positivity: "Will this make me stronger, better, and more efficient?" Do not prolong your deliberation too long, however—learn to decide carefully but at the same time quickly and without dawdling or waste of time. Then, when you have determined upon your course of action—have decided what to do, and how to do it, as well as understanding why you should do it—then proceed to actually do it with all your might. Follow the old maxim: "Be sure you're right, then go ahead!"

Hold the wild horses of your mentality firmly in hand, using the guiding reins of the reason and judgment—but see that they go ahead!

4. Cultivate the Attention. Carefully cultivate the Attention until you can focus it upon any object or subject with concentrated force and insistent direction. The Attention determines the path of the will—either toward or away from the object of the Attention, as the case may be. Attention is the eye of the Ego, or Master Mind, the driver of the mental chariot. Note the following quotations from leading psychologists on this point: "The first and great task of the will is the control and direction of the Attention. The will determines the kind of interest that shall prevail at the moment, and the kind of interest largely determines the character of the man, his tastes, his feelings, his thoughts, his acts."

"Cooperating with a pre-existing influence, the will can make a weaker motive prevail over a stronger. It determines which of pre-existing influences shall have control over the mind."

"If the will relaxes its hold over the activities of the mind, the Attention is liable to be carried away by any one of the thousands of ideas that the laws of association are constantly bringing

351

into our minds."

5. Acquire the Habit of Mastery. Carefully cultivate and acquire the habit of controlling your mental faculties, feelings, desires, and thoughts, as well as your actions, by the power of your awakened will. When you have acquired this habit— and the mental faculties have discovered your power over them, and they also have acquired the habit of obeying—half the battle is over. Then will the wild horses of the mind have learned the lesson of control, and will interpose a constantly decreasing degree of resistance, and they will manifest a constantly increasing obedience. Don't allow your mental steeds to run away with the chariot. They will do wonderful work if properly controlled and directed, but if they are permitted to rush along unrestrained by and heedless of the hand of the Master Mind, they will run into mire and morass, and may even wreck the chariot and throw the charioteer into the ditch or over the precipice. Habit becomes second nature, remember—and habit is strengthened by repetition. So keep at it, and your power of control will increase daily, and their response and obedience will increase in like proportion.

6. Occasionally Perform Disagreeable Tasks. You will find that it is of great benefit to oc-

casionally drive your mental steeds in directions contrary to that in which they wish to travel. This course is advisable, not because the agreeable way is necessarily wrong, but simply because such exercise of control trains them and accustoms them to the control and direction of the Master Mind. One of the best methods of Mind Mastery is to compel yourself to occasionally perform some disagreeable task, something you do not wish to do, or do not feel like doing. Here you will have a fight worthy of the mettle of the Master Mind. The rebellious feelings and desires will rear and plunge and use every art and wile in order to defeat your purpose. Finding that you are determined to rule, they may even seem to acquiesce for the time being, only to afterward take you by surprise and off your guard when you relax your efforts and rest secure in the feeling that you have conquered. They sometimes act like the mule in the well-known story of Josh Billings, the American humorist; this mule, he said, would sometimes stay good for three months just to get a chance to kick the hostler when he wasn't expecting it.

Desires and feelings are wily animals—watch them and do not be caught napping or off your guard. By doing a few disagreeable things once in a while—doing something that you do not feel like doing, or leaving undone some thing you do feel like doing, you will gain a wonderful control over your emotional nature, and desire-mind, that will serve you well in some future hour of need when you require every available ounce of your Will Power in order to act right. Moreover, by following this course, you will educate your mental faculties in the direction of acquiring the habit of yielding to the control and mastery of the will—that is to say, of course, to the Will directed by the Master Mind or Ego. Many great men know this law, and apply it to their advantage. One writer mentions the case of a man who was found reading a particular "dry" work on political economy. His friend expressed surprise at his choice of a book, and the man replied: "I am doing this because I dislike it!" He was training his mortal horses. One of the best and simplest methods of putting this rule into practice is that of heeding the popular adage: "DO IT NOW!" Procrastination is a particularly balky horse, and one that requires careful and persistent attention.

A writer says on this point: "Nothing schools the will, and renders it ready for effort in this complex world, better than accustoming it to face disagreeable things. Professor James advises all to do something occasionally for no other reason than that they would rather not do it, if it is nothing more than giving up a seat in a street car. He likens such effort to the insurance that a man carries on his house. He has something to fall back on in time of trouble. A will schooled in this way is always ready to respond, no matter how great the emergency. While another would be crying over spilled milk, the possess of such a will has already found another cow. The only way to secure such a will is to practice doing disagreeable things. There are daily opportunities. Such a man has the elements of success in him. On the other hand, the one who habitually avoids disagreeable action is training his will to be of no use to him at a time when supreme effort is demanded. Such a will can never elbow its way to the front in life. We gradually make our characters by separate acts of will, just as the blacksmith by repeated blows beats out a horseshoe or an anchor from a shapeless mass or iron. A finished anchor or horseshoe was never the product of a single blow."

The "James' Formulas"
No presentation of the best modern thought concerning the Cultivation of Will Power would be complete without mention of the celebrated Formulas of the great American psychologist, the late William James. Professor James based these formulas upon those of Bain, elaborating

the latter and adding some equally good advice to them. Here follows a condensed statement of the "James' Formulas," including a condensation of those of Bain which are quoted by James.

1. "In the acquisition of a new habit, or the leaving off of an old one, launch yourself with as strong and decided an initiative as possible. This will give your new beginning such a momentum that the temptation to break down will not occur as soon as it otherwise might; and every day during which a breakdown is postponed adds to the chances of it not occurring at all."

2. "Never suffer an exception to occur till the new habit is securely rooted in your life. Every lapse is like the letting fall of a ball of string which one is carefully winding up—a single slip undoes more than a great many turns will wind again." "It is necessary, above all things, in such a situation, never to lose a battle. Every gain on the wrong side undoes the effect of many conquests on the right. The essential precaution is so to regulate the two opposing powers that the one may have a series of uninterrupted successes, until repetition has fortified it to such a degree as to enable it to cope with the opposition, under any circumstances."

3. "Seize the very first possible opportunity to act on every resolution you make, and on every emotional prompting you may experience in the direction of the habits you wish to gain. It is not the moment of their forming, but in the moment of their producing motor effects, that resolves, and aspirations communicate their new 'set' to the brain. The actual presence of the practical opportunity alone furnishes the fulcrum upon which the lever can rest, by which the moral will may multiply its strength and raise itself aloft. He who has no solid ground to press against will never get beyond the stage of empty gesture making."

4. "Keep the faculty alive in you by a little gratuitous exercise every day. That is, be systematically ascetic or heroic in little, unnecessary points; do every day something for no other reason than that you would rather not do it, so that when the hour of dire need draws nigh, it may find you not unnerved and untrained to stand the test. The man who has daily inured himself to habits of concentrated attention, energetic volition, and self-denial in unnecessary thing will stand like a tower when everything rocks around him, and when his softer mortals are winnowed like chaff in the blast."

Inspiring Ideals. The student who is striving to develop his Will Power will do well to hold before his mental vision the Inspiring Ideal of the Goal toward which he is struggling and striving. The following quotations from well-known writers will perhaps serve the student well in this regard. Let him commit some of these quoted lines to memory, and frequently repeat them to himself, and thus create a Living Ideal which will stimulate and inspire him to continued and renewed effort—this will aid him greatly in the work of making the Ideal become REAL. Here follow the said quotations:

The star of the unconquered will,

It rises in my breast,

Serene and resolute and still,

And calm and self-possessed.

So nigh is grandeur to our dust,

So near to God is man,

When duty whispers low, "Thou must!"

The youth replies, "I can!"

"The longer I live, the more certain I am that the great difference between men, between the feeble and the powerful, the great and the insignificant, is energy— invincible determination— a purpose once fixed, and then death or victory. That quality will do anything that can be done in this world, and no talents, no circumstances, no opportunities will make a two-legged creature a man without it."

"Resolve is what makes a man manifest; not puny resolve, not crude determination, not errant purpose, but that strong and indefatigable will which treads down difficulties and danger as a boy treads down the heaving frost lands of winter, which kindles his eye and brain with a proud pulse beat toward the unattainable. Will makes men giants."

"Let the fools prate of luck. The fortunate is he whose earnest purpose never swerves, Whose slightest action, or inaction, serves the one great aim. Why, even death itself stands still and waits an hour sometimes for such a will."

"I have brought myself by long meditation to the conviction that a human being with a settled purpose must accomplish it, and that nothing can resist a will which will stake even existence upon its fulfillment."

"A passionate desire and an unwearied will can perform impossibilities, or what may seem to be such to the cold and feeble."

"It is wonderful how even the casualties of life seem to bow to a spirit that will not bow to them, and yield to subserve a design which may, in their first apparent tendency, threaten to frustrate. When a firm, decisive spirit is recognized, it is curious to see how the space clears around a man and leaves him room and freedom."

"I am bigger than anything that can happen to me. All these things are outside my door, and I've got the key! Man was meant to be, and ought to be, stronger and more than anything that can happen to him. Circumstances, 'Fate,' 'Luck,' are all outside; and if he cannot change them, he can always beat them!"

"Man owes his growth chiefly to that active striving of the will—that encounter which we call effort—and it is astonishing to find how often results apparently impracticable are thus made possible. It is Will—force of purpose—that enables a man to do or be whatever he sets his mind upon being or doing. Let it be your first duty to teach the world that you are not wood and straw—that there is some iron in you."

Tender-handed stroke a nettle,

And it stings you for your pains.

Grasp it like a man of mettle,

And it soft as down remains

Parting Words

And now, my good reader, we have come to the end of this book. Its pages are filled with information of vital importance to you—information which will make your character what you wish it to be, providing that you so Will it, and providing that you will back up that Will with persistent, determined purpose and effort. I can do no more for you, however, than to point out the way for you to travel—you must tread the path yourself, for no one else can tread it for you.

Decide which you wish to be: Master Mind or Slave Mind! You have the choice— make it! I have led you to the spring from which bubbles the Waters of Mastery—but I cannot force you to drink thereof. In the words of an old writer: "Man must be either the Anvil or the Hammer—let each make his choice, and then complain not."

If you are the Hammer, strike your fill

If, the Anvil, stand you still

Other Titles by
Janice & Mel's
Life Transformation Publishing
www.lifetransformationpublishing.com

As a Man Thinketh — ~~Scripty~~
by James Allen   *see pg 53*
                    TMM

As a Woman Thinks
by James Allen & Janice Demano

As a Man Thinks
by James Allen & Mel Waller

As a Man Thinks Large Print Edition
by James Allen & Mel Waller

The Way of Peace
by James Allen

The Path of Prosperity
by James Allen

The Mastery of Destiny
by James Allen

The Heavenly Life
by James Allen

Entering the Kingdom
by James Allen

Byways of Blessedness
by James Allen

Above Life's Turmoil
by James Allen

Eight Pillars of Prosperity
by James Allen

Foundation Stones to Happiness and Success
by James Allen

From Passion to Peace
by James Allen

Light on Life's Difficulties
by James Allen

Man: King of Mind, Body and Circumstance
by James Allen

Men and Systems
by James Allen

Morning and Evening Thoughts
by James Allen

Out From the Heart
by James Allen

The Divine Companion
by James Allen

The Life Triumphant:
Mastering the Heart and Mind
by James Allen

The Shining Gateway
by James Allen

Through the Gates of Good
Or Christ and Conduct
by James Allen

Think and Grow Rich
by Napoleon Hill

The Master Mind
by Theron Q Dumont

New Titles being added regularly!